Autism Talks and Talks

Book 4 of the School Daze Series

Dr. Sharon A. Mitchell

Other books in the series:

Autism Goes to School

Autism Runs Away

Autism Belongs

Autism Talks & Talks

Autism Grows Up

Autism Boxed Set

Coming soon - *Autism Goes to School Workbook*

Coming soon - *Prequel to Autism Goes to School*

This is a work of fiction, a figment of the author's imagination. Any resemblance to real people or events is coincidental. This story is for entertainment and information purposes only. The author assumes no responsibility for the strategies or suggestions described.

Copyright © 2016 Sharon A. Mitchell

All rights reserved.

ISBN: 0988055392
ISBN-13: 978-0-9880553-9-1

DEDICATION

To Devon who shows over and over that it can be done.

Sharon A. Mitchell

Contents

CHAPTER 1	1
CHAPTER 2	6
CHAPTER 3	11
CHAPTER 4	16
CHAPTER 5	26
CHAPTER 6	30
CHAPTER 7	38
CHAPTER 8	46
CHAPTER 9	53
CHAPTER 10	61
CHAPTER 12	79
CHAPTER 13	86
CHAPTER 14	93
THANK YOU	97
Other Books in the Series	98
Autism Goes to School	98
Autism Runs Away	100
Autism Belongs	101
Autism Grows Up	103

Autism Goes to School Workbook 105

Prequel to Autism Goes to School 105

ACKNOWLEDGMENTS

Thanks to MEL, the greatest team of editors ever.

Cover design by Rachel of Littera Designs.

CHAPTER 1

Lori's back was to the door as she put away the last of the staff coffee cups. Everyone was supposed to clean up after themselves, but that didn't always happen. The kitchen needed to be tidy before the kids arrived.

"Who are you?" a strange man asked from the doorway. In his hands were bulging plastic grocery bags.

"I'm Lori Nabaker. Who are you supposed to be?" Although school was over for the day, the doors off the parking lot were open for kids to arrive. But, anyone could walk in.

"Supposed to be?" The guy just stared at her, the bags dangling from his fingertips. "What do you mean 'supposed to be'? I am who I am; there's no supposing about it." He looked at her some more. "Are you *supposed* to be here?"

Lori's weirdo meter rose. What was with this guy? Who was he and how'd she get trapped in this room with him? Never show fear and maybe she could bluff her way out. "Excuse me. Let me pass." His large body still blocked the doorway. Then he stood aside, taking a step into the room and pivoting so that the back of his hips pressed against the counter's edge.

As she scurried out the door, away from this strange man, she heard him mutter, "Mel should have warned me about the odd people here. At least she'll be out of the way before the kids get here."

Lori stopped. "Kids? Mel?"

"You know my sister?"

"Mel's your sister?"

When the guy nodded, the tension in Lori's shoulders dropped noticeably. She came back into the room with her hand extended. "You must be Jeff - Mel's told me about you. I'm the EA who works in her classroom sometimes." Jeff looked blankly at her, so she explained. "EA. You know, Educational Associate. I help out with the kids."

There was no recognition in his eyes and his expression didn't change. Come to think of it, his expression hadn't changed since he arrived. But his next words were gentler. "Oh, yeah, Mel told me that someone from the school would assist me."

"Assist you? I thought *I* was running the Little Chef's club and that Mel's brother was supposed to assist me."

"There you go with that suppose thing again." Jeff looked away from her as he laid the things from his grocery bags on the counter. Each item was lined up precisely, equal distance from each other and from the edge of the counter. Concentrating on his task, Jeff asked, "Are you a chef?"

His words were muffled partly because his back was to her and partly because he was dragging packages along the counter, getting their placement just right. "Pardon," she asked. "What did you say?"

"I said, 'Are you a chef?'".

"I just told you I'm an EA."

"Well, then..."

"Well, then what?"

"Well, then, I *am* a chef. That's why Mel asked me to volunteer my time to run the Little Chef's club. You can help me though, that is, if you know how to act and don't scare the kids. If you stay you're going to have to watch your language."

"My language!" Lori's indignation made her voice rise on the last syllable. She most certainly had not used any profanity during this whole unpleasant encounter.

"Yes, your language. You'll have to watch how you talk around the kids. No more of this "suppose" stuff. You have to speak plainly and say what you mean. Some of the kids who'll be here have autism, you know. They won't like your imprecise way of talking."

As Lori's mouth opened in retort, there was a flurry of rustling plastic as Mel came through the door carrying far more bags than the two Jeff had arrived with.

Mel dropped the bags on the floor and smiled at both of them. "Oh, good," she said. "I see that you've already met."

Her smile froze as she looked from Jeff to Lori and back again. "Hey, guys, is everything all right?"

Jeff reached for the bags and continued the tedious process of unpacking and lining up the contents perfectly on the counter.

"It's a good thing the counter's long," Lori said, the sarcasm sneaking into her voice. Mel gave her a sharp look, but Jeff simply agreed. "Yep."

Sensing the tension, Mel asked, "What's going on?"

Her brother answered, "We were just getting a few things straight.

We've established that Lori's an EA and I'm a chef."

Mel continued looking from her brother to her friend. "So, why is that a problem?"

"No problem," Lori hurried to reassure her. "We're good."

Sneakers squeaked and slapped on the hallway floor, accompanied by high-pitched voices. The kids had arrived for Little Chef Club.

"Well, this is it," said Lori.

"What is it?" Jeff asked.

"The beginning of Little Chefs."

Jeff stared at her. "What did you think it would be?" Then, turning to his sister, "Are you sure she's the right person to be helping us with this? She seems unclear about a number of things."

Mel squeezed his shoulder. "Wait until you see her with the kids. You'll see that she's perfect."

Jeff didn't look convinced but the kids burst through the door, overtaking any conversation the adults had begun. The students' enthusiasm was admirable but needed to be toned down to match the size of the school's kitchen. Mel had them line up against the wall. She waited for silence before reminding the group who she was, then introducing Lori and Jeff.

"How can you be a chef?" one boy asked. "Where's your chef's hat?"

"Right here." Jeff pulled it out of the last bag and settled it on his head. Next, he donned his apron, pulling the string ties from the back and fastening them in the front.

"Wow! Just like on TV," said Matt, the smallest child in the line.

"Not necessarily," said Karen, a grade six student. "It depends on the restaurant and on the show. There are all kinds of aprons and several kinds of chef hats. First, there's..."

"Thanks, Karen," Mel interrupted. "We might have time to go into that later, but right now we need to begin our chef's session. Jeff will be leading our group since he's an actual chef"

Over Mel's head, Jeff grinned at Lori. To the kids he said, "Who washed their hands before coming here?"

Of the eight kids, two put up their hands.

"Good for you. Now, we're going to do it all over again."

Groans came from several kids, along with "Do we have to?" "Again?" "Mine look okay already."

"Anyone who touches anything or eats in my kitchen must first wash their hands," Jeff announced. "Ms. Nabaker will show you how."

When Lori hesitated, he asked Mel, "She does know how, doesn't she?" This made the kids laugh, Jeff look at them quizzically and Lori glare at him before herding the kids in a line towards the sink.

Standing beside his sister, out of the way of the line-up, Jeff said, "I think this is starting off all right."

"Mostly. Except for Lori. You're being a little hard on her, aren't you?"

"What do you mean? She has to wash her hands just like everybody else. She wants to help lead, so I thought this was something she could be in charge of." He waited a minute then asked, "Why aren't you getting in line?"

While Mel waited her turn, she listened to the kids. One voice rose above the others, both in volume and frequency. Karen was explaining to anyone who would listen, the different hand washing techniques. She was currently at the sink demonstrating how a surgeon would wash, counting off the number of scrubs for each finger. Except no one was paying any attention to her monologue.

A grade six boy, Jim said, "Come on, Karen. We're never going to get to cook anything if you hog the sink the whole time." Lori intervened and got the line moving again.

When Karen's voice continued to rise above the others about this hand washing business, Mel intervened. "You certainly know a lot about hand washing, Karen. Thanks for your input, but we're moving on now to the cooking part."

Karen paused then switched topics. "Chateaubriand is made from the most expensive cut of beef. It's cut from the tenderloin and is about four inches thick." The other kids just looked at her as she continued. "Because of the thickness of the cut and how expensive the meat is, it has to be cooked just right."

Again, Mel interrupted. "Thanks, Karen, but we're not talking about Chateaubriand this week."

"But it's a classic chef dish," Karen protested.

Jeff took over. "Right. It is and it's something I make at the deli. But we don't have enough time today or the budget for that kind of meat. Today, we're starting with the basics."

"Basics? But I'm not a basic kind of girl. I know a lot about this stuff already," protested Karen.

As if he hadn't heard her, Jeff continued. "First, we'll learn about safety in the kitchen. Washing your hands and keeping utensils and surfaces clean is key. That comes before anything else, even tasting the food."

"We do get to taste some stuff, don't we?" asked another boy.

"Definitely. It's a poor chef who doesn't taste what he's cooking. How else would you know if it's any good?" The kids looked relieved.

"Who has used a knife before?" Jeff asked. Most kids raised a hand. Jeff pulled a foot long knife from the drawer. "Who has used a knife like this?"

"That's a cimeter and used for butchering, but not normal kitchen use," Karen informed them. "Sometimes it's used for cutting steaks and tenderloin, the kind used in Chateaubriand."

Jeff looked at her. "Are you here to learn or to teach?"

Lori moved to Karen's side and placed an arm along her shoulder. "Karen reads a lot and stores her knowledge. Cooking shows are her passion, so she has a lot to offer this group." She smiled at her warmly.

"I watch a lot of cooking shows too, and study this area. But we're not here to spout off our knowledge. We're here to learn how to cook certain items that I've chosen. If you want to discuss some aspects of cooking with me after class that will be fine." Jeff's words were blunt, but only Lori seemed uncomfortable.

Over Karen's head, Mel grinned at Lori. She mouthed, "It's okay," then nodded at Karen. Mel was right; Karen did not look upset or show that she might have felt snubbed.

CHAPTER 2

The class went well, at least as far as Lori could tell, despite her misgivings about Jeff. The kids did not seem to notice the little things that bothered Lori. The kids didn't mind Jeff's dictatorial methods; they actually looked to him for leadership. Lori was surprised at how Mel allowed Jeff to take the lead as well. Maybe she knew her brother and trusted him. Maybe there was more to Jeff than Lori's initial impression suggested.

The parents trickled in to collect their offspring. Above the clamor, Karen's voice rang clear. At times she tried to engage Jeff or Mel; at other times, it seemed that she just talked. It didn't seem to matter if anyone responded or if her conversation connected to that of the kids or adults around her. Every so often Jeff responded to something Karen said and they carried on a discussion of their own. No one else heeded these conversations.

Rita Blackwell, Karen's mother appeared at the door. She grimaced at Lori and Mel and said in a low voice, " I could hear my daughter all the way down the hall." She nodded towards Karen. "Has she been all right? Has she been annoying anyone?"

Mel reassured her that Karen had been just fine and that they enjoyed having her. The relief in Rita's face was palpable. "I was so worried," she said.

"Why?" Mel asked as she stepped out into the hallway, away from the others.

Rita followed her. "I guess I should have been upfront about this before sending Karen, but she so wanted to come as soon as she heard that there would be a Little Chef's club. Cooking is her passion, but you might have gathered that."

Lori's wry grin and nod assured her that they had not missed that fact.
"She can go overboard when she likes something. She's intense."
Lori and Mel waited.

Rita looked uncomfortable. "I know that she can go on and on about whatever interests her at the time. It's hard to get a word in edge wise. But, she really does study things and she knows so much."

From the kitchen, they could hear Karen, back on the subject of Chateaubriand.

Rita grimaced. "You may have guessed that she likes cooking shows. She gets impatient with her father and I because we can't talk about cooking the way she would like. And, we get impatient with her because she can talk incessantly." She hesitated. "How did you manage with her in the group?"

Lori rushed to reassure her. "It was just fine. We didn't always answer her questions, but Jeff handled the group well."

Lori surprised herself on that one, but thinking back, it was true. Despite his bluntness, Jeff had managed the kids, even convincing them that roasted root vegetables would be a marvelous dish to make and eat. In the end, the kids had loved it. The older ones were shown proper knife handling techniques and peeled and chopped the parsnips, carrots, onions and squash into uniform, diagonal pieces. The younger kids had used a crinkle cut safety blade to chop vegetables, giving them a serpentine edge. Then they all got to dig their hands into bowls of vegetables, coating them liberally with oil and freshly chopped herbs. The aroma was tantalizing and even those who said they hated vegetables dug in once they came out of the oven. Jeff had grinned at Lori, reminding them both of her objections when she'd realized that veggies would be the focus of their first cooking class.

Rita looked down then peered from Mel to Lori. "Look," she said. "I suppose I should tell you." She sighed. "My daughter is not normal."

Lori tried to reassure her that Karen was a lovely child, but a look from Mel silenced her. Mel stood quietly waiting, her expression neutral, her eyes not leaving Rita's face. They waited.

"You see," Rita continued, "Karen has a syndrome. It's called Asperger's syndrome. That's why she does what she does - she can't help it." She looked from Lori to Mel, trying to gauge their reactions. Lori took her cue from Mel and said nothing.

To fill the dead air space, Rita hurried on, her words spilling out. "But she's really smart, you know. Really, really smart. She knows lots of things, things most kids her age would never dream of. That's typical of kids with Asperger's. They're also highly verbal and often talk and talk. It's okay to talk sometimes, but Karen does not know when to stop. She will go on and on and on, even when her audience has walked away.

"And she annoys people. She doesn't give them a chance to talk. And she doesn't care what they want to talk about. It only matters what's on her mind. She comes across as selfish and a know-it-all. But honest, she's not trying to brag or even to bore you. It's just that she finds things fascinating and her latest interest is cooking. You would not believe how much she can talk." There was a pause. "Sort of like me, huh? I guess I've just done the same thing and you're probably thinking that Karen comes by this honest enough. Sorry." The last was said in a small voice. "I'll collect my kid and we'll leave you in peace."

"Wait." Lori put a hand on her arm. "We know about Asperger's and this club is perfect for kids just like Karen."

Mel agreed that yes, Karen had talked a lot, especially at the beginning of the sessions. She explained to Rita that with guidance and correction, Karen was able to restrain herself and speak at appropriate times. She added, "Being highly verbal, yes, is frequently a part of AS."

Rita looked surprised that Mel knew the acronym.

"Yes, I'm quite familiar with Asperger's Syndrome, as is Lori here and so is our chef, Jeff. In fact, Jeff may be even more familiar with it than you are."

"And it's still all right that Karen comes again?"

"Most definitely," Lori assured her.

"Having AS is all the more reason that she should come."

"She didn't drive the other kids crazy with all her chattering?"

"To be honest, at times yes, some of the other children were annoyed."

"I'm so sorry. I hope they weren't mean to her. She gets her feelings hurt so easily and she doesn't mean to be rude."

"Does it matter whether or not her intention is to be rude if she comes across that way?"

"What do you mean?" Rita asked.

Lori tried to explain. "If you are trying to be rude, people won't want to be around you." The next part she said gently. "If you are rude, even without intending to be, people still won't want to be around you."

Rita's shoulders sagged. "That happens to my little girl all the time. She starts out all right and often kids are accepting at first. But then she talks too long and doesn't let them have a turn and you can see the kids give up on her and just go away. Then Karen's left all alone without a clue how things turned out that way and she's so sad. Sometimes she tries to hide it by saying the kids are mean and stupid and she doesn't care."

"What do you do about it?" Mel asked.

"Do? What do you mean?" asked Rita. "I have no control over other people's children."

"True, but you do have control over your own." She grimaced. "Well, at least some control. As I mentioned, I have a son and I'm humbled to admit just how little control I do have. He seems to have a mind of his own." She smiled proudly. "Sometimes, that's what I love most about him."

"He really is a sweetie," Lori agreed. She turned to Rita. "But, life is a group affair and we all have to be able to function in a group. That's part of the reason we're having Little Chef's Club - to help kids learn to be a part of a group."

"Karen's an individual," her mother said.

"Yep, and that's what's delightful about all of the kids. They all have unique personalities and idiosyncrasies, strengths and challenges."

"Karen's strength is her brain and her interests. She knows so much and is far brighter than any of the other kids."

"Do you know the other kids in the group?" Mel's eyes were steely.

"Well, no, but I do know how smart my Karen is."

Lori had seen that look in Mel's eyes before. Ever the peace keeper, she dove in. "What Mel's trying to say is that being smart isn't good enough."

Rita looked skeptical. " My daughter is really very smart. That's the greatest thing she has going for her. Sometimes I fear that that's the *only* thing she has going for her."

"But what's the point in being smart if you can't use it?"

"What do you mean?" asked Rita.

Lori explained. "Say that Karen keeps this interest in cooking, grows up and tries to find a job in a kitchen. How would she be received if she entered the restaurant talking the way she is now? How would the head chef respond to the new hire telling him what to do?"

"Maybe Karen would be right and her ideas were better than what the chef was already doing," her mother protested.

"She might well have some great ideas and lots to contribute to that restaurant, but do you think the management is going to listen to Karen, this kid's first night on the job? Would she even last her first day without being fired?

Rita's shoulders sagged. "I see what you mean. We get so scared for her. She has unlimited potential but she turns people off without meaning to." Then an idea struck her. "Maybe we could buy a restaurant and have Karen run it."

"Would Karen be the only person there? Wouldn't there be sous chefs and servers and dishwashers - all people Karen would need to interact with and get along with? It's pretty hard to escape people, no matter what your job."

"She could stay home and cook for us, I guess."

"Is that the kind of life you envision for your daughter?" Mel asked.

"No, but I don't know what's going to become of her."

"We understand," Mel said. "That's part of the reason we started Little Chef. Some of the kids here are simply interested in learning how to prepare some food. Others are here because they have a hard time fitting into some of the other recreational opportunities out there for kids. You may have noticed that most clubs focus on sports skills. Unfortunately, some kids are just not budding athletes. Others may have the gross motor coordination to play the sport but become overwhelmed by the rules and the observations required to work effectively as a team.

Karen looked relieved that someone understood. "That's Karen."

"And my son," Mel told her.

"Your son?"

"Yes, well, actually my step-son. And some of the other kids here struggle with the social aspects of being part of a group. That's why we have three adults here. We circulate among the kids, coaching and guiding, but for the most part, the initiative is taken by the Little Chef leader, Jeff."

"The guy in the chef hat?" Rita asked.

From the kitchen, now that everyone but Karen and Jeff had left, they could hear the discussion about which sauce was better with Chateaubriand - a Bercy or a Bernaise.

When he bluntly shut her down earlier, in what Lori thought was a rude way, Jeff had promised to talk with Karen later about Chateaubriand. He'd kept his promise, Lori marveled. He hadn't just blown Karen off, but had intended to devote time to her at the end. And he was speaking to Karen in a patient way, yet he didn't sound condescending. He listened and responded and corrected and respected her opinions. Hmmm. Maybe there was more to Jeff than she'd thought. He did have an idea of what he was doing with these kids after all.

CHAPTER 3

As the kids trickled into the kitchen for the next Little Chef's Club, there were some new faces. Karen was the first student to arrive and her voice rose above the others. She immediately washed her hands, and then helped Jeff with the preparations. After watching momentarily, she knew what to do to help without being told. The girl's ability to work with her hands was impressive, especially while she talked non-stop about other aspects of cooking.

Jeff appeared not to be listening and never once glanced Karen's way, yet he made appropriate comments from time to time. When he wanted to make sure Karen heard him, he stood directly in front of her without budging until she looked up at him.

In Lori's mind, things were off to a good start. This time there was no altercation between her and Jeff - partly because Lori was determined to get along, partly because Jeff seemed oblivious to the fact that there had been discord between them the last time and partly because of Karen's presence. Lori was aware of the example they must set for the kids. She was unsure if that thought crossed Jeff's mind. She suspected that he was going to do what he was going to do regardless of who was present.

Two of the grade 6 boys entered the door together, laughing and bumping shoulders. One stopped in his tracks as soon as he saw Karen.

"Who let *her* in here? Ah, geez. If I'd known *Karen* would be here, I wouldn't have come. This sucks. She'll ruin everything."

Jeff was immediately in his face. "Who are you?" he asked.

Steve took a step back and gave his name.

"Do you think you're coming to Little Chef?" Jeff asked.

"Well, I was, but I didn't know *she'd* be here. It'll be no fun now. She never shuts up."

Lori moved to Karen and put an arm around her. Karen stood frozen and for once, silent. She seemed unaware of Lori's presence; her eyes were fixed on Jeff and Steve.

"Whose kitchen is this?" Jeff asked Steve.

"Well, the school's I guess."

Jeff cut him off before he'd finished saying the word school. "It's mine. During Little Chef Club, this is *my* kitchen. Mine alone and I'm in charge." He looked around at the rest of the group who were as still as if they were playing frozen tag. "Any objections?"

No one moved. No one said a word.

Jeff turned back to Steve. "My kitchen, my rules." He paused and his glance took in every person in the room. "In my kitchen, we have respect. We respect the chef, we respect his helper," he nodded at Lori, "and we respect each other. We all have a job to do here. We are all welcome, wanted and needed. *Especially* my number one helper, the person with the most knowledge and experience - Karen. Today's Little Chef would not even be happening without the work she's done for the last half hour getting things ready for kids like you."

He let that sink in. "Those are my rules. Can you live with them? If you can, come on in. If you can't, leave." He turned his back on Steve and returned to the sink. "Karen, would you finish sharpening the knives, please?" He handed Karen the largest butcher knife he had, then turned his back, confident she would get on with the job.

Lori let her breath out. Crisis averted. By the glare on Jeff's face when he first turned on Steve, she thought she might have to intervene to save the offending child from Jeff's wrath. Then she thought she'd have to take Karen out of the room to calm her down and help her recover. But assigning her a job to do and a prestigious job in the kids' minds was the right thing to do. Karen saved face and her position in the group was elevated. Plus, Karen sharpened the knife without uttering a word, her concentration intense, the stainless steel of the twelve inch blade flashing and glittering in glow of the fluorescent lights as she worked.

"A stir-fry requires more work in preparation than it does in the actual cooking. Lots of cutting is involved and I mean precise cutting. Who remembers our knife lesson from last week?" Jeff had their attention.

A few hands went up, some raised higher than others. The kids remembered that wielding a knife was harder than it looked.

"Karen, I remember that you caught on to this quite well. Will you demonstrate for us the proper way to hold your knife and to cut an onion?"

Karen made it look easy. Jeff nodded in satisfaction. "Now, Karen, Lori and I will each work with one of you on knife handling while the rest of you watch. Steve, you're with Karen, Kyle's with Lori and Sam, you'll work with me. Gather round so you can all see." When Steve hesitated, Jeff touched his shoulder and moved him towards Karen's cutting board. Neither Karen nor Steve looked at each other as Karen picked up the knife, demonstrated a few strokes then handed the knife to Steve.

"Here. You try it," she told Steve. She stopped him right away with a reminder to keep the fingers of his other hand out of the way. Then she added a few encouraging words as Steve's strokes became more accurate and his speed gradually picked up.

Lori watched closely, ready to intervene and worried about Jeff's idea of pairing up those two.

Before the activity went on too long, Jeff called the group back and the stir-frying lesson continued.

"Why do we wait for the oil to just start to smoke?" he asked. As Karen opened her mouth to speak, Jeff interrupted. "Let's see. Who hasn't answered in a while?" and chose another student.

Lori liked the way Jeff guided the student towards the right answer, and then beamed at him as if the little boy had come up with the idea all on his own.

When the paper plates and forks were distributed and the kids were sampling their wares, Jeff asked their thoughts on their creations. Once again, even those kids who swore they hated vegetables were tucking in.

"Any problems you can identify with this food?" Jeff asked?

"It's these forks. I can't stab the carrots with it."

Jeff nodded. "Why do you think that is?"

"They're too hard," one student offered.

"Yeah, they're crunchy. I have to pick them up with my fingers."

Another kid said, "I tried scooping them up with my fork but it didn't quite work out." They'd witnessed the elusive carrot skitter across his plate and across the floor.

When the laughter died down, Jeff asked, "Why do we need to make sure all the vegetable pieces are the same size?"

"So that they take the same amount of time to cook" came the answer.

"Are the carrots cooked as much as the other vegetables?"

"No," came from several kids, but Karen said, "Some are and some aren't."

"Right. And why might that be?"

The kids knew the answer. "Because some are bigger than others."

"Whose job was it to cut the carrots?"

Oh no, Lori thought. Please, please Jeff, don't go there. We've had a peaceful half hour; don't ruin things.

When no one answered immediately, Jeff repeated the question.

"Mine," a small voice said. Every head turned to look at Steve.

Jeff's expression was stern. "What do you have to say about this, Steve?"

"Ah, sorry?" came the hesitant reply.

Jeff just looked at him, waiting. Steve opened his mouth to say more, but was cut off by Karen.

"Wait! That's not fair. Steve just started to learn how to use a knife. This was his first time. I was not very good at it the first time I tried, but I've practiced lots. Look at your plates. Not all the pieces are undercooked; some Steve cut just right."

Jeff didn't smile, but just nodded. "Would the rest of you agree with Karen?"

There were nods all around.

"Karen, did you make the right choice in picking Steve to cut the carrots?"

No! No, no, no! What was with this guy's head, Lori thought. Was he trying to create World War III in this kitchen? I've got to step in and salvage what's left of this class. She noticed the tell-tale signs of an impending blow-up with Steve. His shoulders had risen, his teeth were clenched and his hands were becoming balled fists. Before Lori could say anything, Karen spoke.

"Yes. Next to me, Steve's the best cutter, so he was the right choice."

Lori let out her breath and Steve's chin rose from his chest as his shoulders went back down.

"She's right," Jeff said. "For a first try, Steve did a pretty good job, didn't he? Some of his carrot pieces are too big and a few too small but some of them are just right. Good job, Steve. Karen was right to trust you with the hardest cutting task. You'll make a good sous chef if you keep practicing." With hardly a pause, he moved on. "Now, what are your thoughts on the sauce?"

Phew! They dodged that one. Lori could not believe it when Jeff started to criticize Steve's carrot, then her heart dropped when she heard him pull Karen into this. Was he out of his mind? First he paired those two together after the disastrous start to Little Chef's, and then he put Steve on the defensive. From working in his classroom, Lori knew how Steve hated to be told he had done anything wrong.

But it was Karen who saved the day, springing to Steve's defense. On second thought, Lori realized that likely Karen was not defending Steve in particular, but her sense of fair play was affronted. Karen, like many kids with Asperger's Syndrome saw things as they were, in black and white. Karen didn't see this as an opportunity to one-up Steve or get back at him after he publicly humiliated her. No, what she saw was an unfair or inaccurate statement and she automatically corrected it. Karen might not even have been aware that doing so would earn her brownie points with Steve.

Did Jeff know things would work out this way? How could he possibly have orchestrated such a thing? What if Steve had gotten mad? Yikes, they were all in close quarters to knives and hot food. Steve, whether or not he knew it, needed the social skills lessons they'd work on in Little Chef's as much or more than some of the other kids here. What if Steve had stormed out? What if he didn't return? What if he'd blamed Karen, saying she was a lousy teacher and she'd taught him poorly?

As if he felt her eyes on him, Jeff looked over the kids' heads and flashed Lori a wink. Lori colored. Had he read her thoughts? His grin was confident.

He had no training in child development or classroom management the way she did. And people on the autism spectrum were not known for their people skills. Yet, so far Jeff had handled their Little Chef sessions well, managing even the more challenging kids. Whether on purpose or inadvertently, he brought in social skills and drove home his point through cooking, rather than preaching.

Was this just a fluke or did Jeff actually know what he was doing? Had he planned this or was it blind luck?

Initially, Lori's plan was to watch Jeff like a hawk, ready to run interference, defend the kids and rescue the session at any moment. Now, she started watching Jeff for more than just the sake of the students.

CHAPTER 4

As she and Jeff cleaned up after the parents had picked up their kids, Lori thought more about this. Yes, it must have been a fluke that that situation hadn't turned ugly. Jeff just didn't have enough kid-handling experience to have set things out to have such a positive outcome.

Since she was the school staff member here, it was up to her to ensure the well-being of the students. After all, Jeff's chef experience and lessons were only the venue through which the kids were to pick up the much needed social skills. That, after all, was the primary purpose of this club and why these particular kids had been invited to attend, along with a handful or other children.

Just as the carrot criticism had turned out all right, Lori needed a way to broach his handling of the kids with Jeff without getting his back up. Judging by their initial meeting, he could be a prickly guy. Start with a positive, she thought.

"So," she said. "That went pretty well, don't you think?"

"Yep." Jeff remained intent on the soapy water as he washed the woks.

Lori stood, towel at the ready. Okay, that was not a real conversation starter.

"What did you think of how Karen defended Steve?" she asked.

"It was fair."

The pause lengthened. Was he obtuse or did he just not plan on making this easy for her?

Lori, usually the most patient of people, felt her ire rise. "Well, it could have gone south on us."

"South?" Jeff turned and looked towards the blank, south wall of the kitchen.

"You know what I mean."

Jeff just looked at her.

"I mean it could have gone wrong, turned ugly, with Steve feeling badly about himself."

"Well, he should have felt badly. He messed up."

"He's only a kid. Geez Jeff, give him a break. This was his first time."

"And Karen pointed that out to the group."

"Well, it was his first time. Steve has self-esteem issues and tries to compensate by bullying. This could have hurt him."

"But it didn't."

"It could have though."

"But, it didn't. What are you going on about?"

"Like I said, it worked out okay but it could have gone south."

"There you go again," Jeff said. "That imprecise language stuff. I told you that if you're going to work with these kids, you have to use proper language and say what you mean." He returned to the dish washing.

Lori consciously shut her jaw. Imprecise language? Her? Oh, now she got it.

"Going south is an idiom, you know. It means that things could have turned out badly and it might have been hard to recover from that."

"I know. I worked out what you meant, but it would make life easier if you and people like you just said what you meant. Idioms confuse things and I don't want you using them while I'm working with these kids. It takes too much time to explain to them what you were trying to say and I've got a cooking lesson to teach."

Lori could only see his profile while he washed the dishes. He didn't look angry but his words came to her harshly. Few people had ever spoken to Lori this way.

And Lori, usually ever the peace-maker, wanting to please everyone, felt herself responding in kind. Jeff might not be mad, but she was getting that way herself. Lori, who never raised her voice. Lori who never got angry, no matter what the provocation. Well, this same Lori was provoked now.

"Who do you think you are to criticize the way I speak? I'm a trained professional. I've studied child development and behavior management. I'm an intelligent, articulate woman and I know what I'm talking about."

"That's great, but other people would know what you're talking about as well if you would just use plain English."

Grrrr. This man! How could he possibly be related to her friend, Mel? Well, come to think of it, wasn't Mel pretty outspoken, too? But she didn't hurt people's feelings about it.

Lori let out a breath and looked closer at Jeff. No, he wasn't smirking as if he knew he'd just zinged her. In fact, his expression remained neutral. The silence lengthened. Lori fumed and grew more uncomfortable with the dead air space. Jeff did not appear to notice as he handed her the final dish to dry.

She couldn't stand it. "Don't you have anything else to say?" she asked.

"No." Jeff continued to wipe down the sink.

"That's it? We've just going to leave it like this?"

"Yes." He moved on to wiping the counter. "What is your problem?"

Lori's eyes rolled up to peer at her bangs that had frizzed in the heat of the dishwashing. She counted to ten, then fifteen. "Let's start again. I was worried about how things might go with Steve when everyone was down on how he cut the carrots."

"Everyone? There's that imprecise language again."

Lori glared.

Jeff held up his hands. "Look. Steve made a mistake. The mistake was pointed out. Karen explained that the mistake was because Steve is just learning. Fair enough. We moved on and everyone left happy."

"But it could have gone so wrong.."

"Did it?"

"No but..."

"Look, Lori. Give me a little credit for having a brain here. I know about these kids. Don't you think I was like them - the kid who didn't fit in, the kid who didn't seem to get what came easily to everyone else."

Lori waited, the anger slowly draining away.

"You're making some assumptions about me, aren't you? You're prejudiced just because I have Asperger's."

Lori's indignation had her sputtering but Jeff just rolled on.

"You think that because I have Asperger's, I'm insensitive to other people's feelings or that I don't recognize them in these kids. Well, you're wrong. I get it."

Lori tried to speak, but Jeff wasn't finished.

"I resent your assumptions. It's insulting to me, to other people with Asperger's and to these kids. Just because something doesn't come naturally doesn't mean it's impossible to learn. I've worked at this. *You*, Ms. Nabaker have made assumptions. You know what assume means, don't you? Assume makes an ass out of 'u' and me."

Jeff was on a roll.

"Do you expect me to coddle these kids? To make sure everything is sunshine and roses for them?" The side of his mouth turned up. "That's an idiom, you know."

Lori's eyes widened. She wasn't sure if he was serious, making a joke or poking fun at her.

Jeff didn't wait for an answer. "The only way to build these kids' self-esteem is to give them confidence - make them feel that they can learn a new skill and that they're competent."

"There are other ways to build self-esteem."

"Well, this is the only way I know and it worked for me. It's working for Karen and it will work for Steve."

"How can you be so sure?"

"Because I've been there and because I notice what's going on with the kids. You wait until the end of our sessions. These kids will be proud of themselves and they'll have learned useful skills."

That sank in for a few seconds then Lori responded. "Some of these kids have been through so much in their young lives. I worry about them."

"Do you think I don't get that? Do you think I don't know what it's like to be bullied? Consider a guy with Asperger's going through the school system twenty-some years ago before anyone knew much about Asperger's or learning differently. I was the weird guy in the back who was smart like a geek but never fit in. These kids are struggling to find their way as well. I can give them some skills."

Then Jeff added, "Everyone has to eat, right?"

Lori laughed at that. "Okay, but...."

"*Now* what?"

"About my language..."

"That's your responsibility. I've told you what you need to do."

"No, you're wrong."

Jeff's eyebrows raised but he didn't look offended. Come to think of it, she sometimes had a hard time deciding which emotion Jeff was feeling because he didn't show it in his facial expression very often.

"I admit that I do speak in idioms sometimes. But so do most people."

"Yes, that's a problem."

"Not really. It makes our language more colorful and paints a picture of what you want to convey." She interrupted as Jeff started to speak. "Look. Whether or not you like it, idioms are part of our language and our culture. Kids will be exposed to them all the time and need to understand them."

"It would make life simpler if people would just quit using them, but you're right, they are all over the place. People let them creep into conversations all the time."

"My point exactly. We can't shield kids from them and they need to be able to understand them so they don't get confused by the message."

"We could make Little Chef's Club an idiom-free zone and we'd all be happier. I could even make a visual for it for next week." He grinned. "The visual would mainly be for *your* benefit."

"No. This is something the kids need to learn, so I *will* use idioms."

"Even if the kids won't know what you're talking about? It's one thing for me to puzzle it out, but is it fair to the kids to make them guess?"

"We'll try this, then. We'll work on just one or two idioms each week. We'll use them, then explain what they mean and make a point to use them over and over again during the lesson."

"You sound like Mel. She insists on using idioms in front of Kyle, even though he's only seven."

"Yes, she's big on preparing him for the world and says that that preparation starts now."

"She doesn't want what happened to me to happen to him."

"You?" Lori didn't know when she'd seen a more self-confident, take-charge guy.

"Yeah, me. When I was Kyle's age no one knew much about Asperger's or high functioning autism. My parents just knew that something was different and they worried. It came out as protection. Looking back, they put no demands on me - different from the way they raised Mel. I was shielded from everything, but I was smart enough that everyone assumed college would be easy for me."

When he didn't go on, Lori asked, "And was it?"

"No. Yes and no. I raced through the textbooks, at least the ones I didn't find boring. The learning part was no problem but everything else was."

"Ever heard of executive functioning? That's the ability to organize and prioritize and sequence and manage time. I had none of those skills. All those classes and assignments and exams were too much for me to juggle. Plus auditory processing is hard in a crowded lecture theatre, rubbing shoulders with hundreds of other kids. My hearing's fine, but I have to work at understanding the words I hear. It's harder in a noisy or echoes."

"And, to top it all off, people had accommodated me all my life. Teachers accommodated *me*. I took all the time I wanted with assignments in high school. If I didn't hand something in, the teachers knew I knew it and gave me marks for other things I did. At home, the rule was to do whatever keeps Jeff calm and happy."

"Sounds like a charmed life."

"Huh. A make-believe life is more like it. It all hit the fan when I got to college and no one there knew these 'Jeff rules'. There, I was treated like every other student and expected to follow the rules - me, who had had exceptions made for me all my life."

"What did you do?"

"Quit. I dropped out."

"And then what did you do?"

"Lived in my parents' basement. How stereotypical is that?"

"How'd you live? How did you support yourself?"

"If my parents had their way, I would have lived off them forever. But I had some pride. I'm good with computers - very good. I got online gigs for beta testing, regression testing, website development and stuff like that."

"That sounds all right."

"If you like living underground. I fell into the trap of staying up all night working or playing games and sleeping most of the day, like a vampire, never seeing the light of day."

"That can't be healthy."

"Tell me about it. You just get more isolated and depressed even though you're doing something you like."

"You don't seem like that guy now."

"I'm not. And Mel played a part in it. Now I'm a chef in Ellie's bakery during the day. Ellie starts *her* day at four o'clock every morning but I'm not that crazy. I come in hours after her and get ready for the lunch and supper crowds."

"Sounds like it worked out all right."

"My parents were terrified for me and furious with Mel when I started at the bakery, but their over-protectiveness would have done me in. I can't say that I always feel like going to work, but who does? Once I'm there, it's good and I socialize more than I ever thought I would."

"And now you're running Little Chef's and helping kids."

Jeff grinned. "Glad to see you know who's in charge finally."

Lori turned down one corner of her mouth at him. "Now, back to those idioms. Which ones do you want to use next week?"

"Uh huh. I'm not the idiom queen - you are. You pick and let me know which ones. You wanted to help lead this group, so take some responsibility and lead the way with your idioms."

Lori bristled then noticed Jeff's grin. Was he pulling her leg? He was. The guy did have a sense of humor.

Jeff grabbed his coat off the hook and headed for the door. "Come on. Let's get out of here. I'll walk you to your car."

The walk to the parking lot seemed shorter than usual to Lori. Jeff waited while she rummaged in her hand bag for her keys. First she tried while it was slung over her shoulder. Then she let it drop down her arm and held it with one hand while she dug around. Come one, come on. I know you're in here somewhere. She always meant to be one of those organized women who had a purse with a compartment for each thing. She turned and tried holding her purse up to the distant street light.

Suddenly, a tiny bright light flashed in her eyes, then into her bag. "Does this help?" Jeff asked, shining a miniature LED light into the cavern of her bag.

"Where did that come from?"

"I might not carry a suitcase around with me, but I do have pockets, you know."

"It's just that I tossed them in here in a hurry when I got to work this morning. They're not that easy to find, you know."

"I can see that. Having some executive functioning problems, are you?"

"What?"

"Are you having some trouble with your organizational skills? Or maybe it's your short-term memory."

"What are you talking about?" Lori was distracted as she continued to dig through the layers for her keys. "Ah! There they are." There was a beep as she hit the button and her car door unlocked.

"Don't you put your keys in some place where you can find them?"

"Of course I do. They were in my purse."

"I repeat. Don't you put your keys some place where you can find them?"

"Ha, ha. Very funny."

"It was? I wasn't trying to be funny. In case you didn't notice, I was using plain language that would be readily understood."

Lori didn't know if she should laugh, be annoyed, or give Jeff a straight answer. She opted for honesty. "I do need a better system, don't I?"

"Cheer up. You found your keys. For a few minutes I thought your purse was like Mary Poppin's carpet bag."

"What? What's Mary Poppins got to do with a carpet or anything else?"

"Didn't you ever watch that movie when you were a kid? You know, the Chimchiminy song and all that stuff? You're a talker. I bet you could say supercalifragilupusexpialidocious really fast. And maybe even backwards. Dosiousaliexpilupusfragicalirepus."

The last part was said in unison with laughter by Jeff and Lori. "Yep," said Jeff. "I knew you would have known that."

"Thanks for seeing me to my car and for the laugh," said Lori. She looked around at the now empty parking lot. "Where's your car?"

"I walked."

"Hop in and I'll give you a ride."

Lori pulled out of the parking lot. "You'll have to tell me where you live."

"I did."

"You did? Sorry, I must have forgotten. Where do you live again?"

"In my parents' basement."

"Very funny."

"Actually, it's not really funny at all."

Lori looked at Jeff. His face was difficult to see in the dim light of from the dashboard, but what she could see was the gleam of his teeth in his wide-mouthed grin.

"Jerk," she said and smiled back. "Which way to we go to get to your parents' basement?"

After giving the directions, Jeff and Lori rode in silence. The car felt like a cocoon in the still night.

"You know, it actually isn't funny at all," Jeff said.

"What's not funny?" Lori sometimes felt like she was a step behind when conversing with Jeff.

"Living in my parents' basement. It's not funny and it's not fun."

"Why do you live there then?"

"Because that's where my computer is."

Lori looked at him. Was this guy for real?

"Just kidding," Jeff assured her, "although I do have tables full of computers and peripherals there. I guess I stay because it's convenient. I'm lazy. It makes my mother feel better. Inertia. Dislike of change. Pick one, any one and you're probably right."

"Do you have to live there if you don't like it? I mean, you have a job. Can't you afford your own place?"

"Yeah, I could. Quite easily in fact. I've saved a lot of money these last years. I've lived rent-free, don't own a car, and the only things I really spend money on are computer components and other tech stuff."

"So, why don't you move out?"

"I'm thinking about it. I should. You probably have no idea how much I hate change, though."

"So? Change is something we all have to get used to, don't we?"

"Yeah. Things have changed a lot in the past year. Mel met Ben and Kyle, I acquired a nephew and I got a job where I get to put my cooking skills to use."

"Is all this change a good thing?"

"Yeah. I was nervous at first, but yes, it is good. Mostly. Some days I'd rather sleep in and hole up in the basement - just me and my computer screens."

"Screens? Don't you mean screen?"

"What kind of a geek has just one computer monitor?"

"Sorry, sorry." Lori apologized. "I didn't mean to insult your geekiness." She continued, "Have you always lived there?"

"When we were kids, Mel and I had bedrooms upstairs. I lived in a dorm during my disaster of a first year of college. When I dropped out of school I left the dorm and moved back home. Then I started accumulating more and more computer stuff until my room was too full. So, I set everything up in the basement. Since I would work through the night I'd just crash there when I got tired. Gradually all my stuff came downstairs with me and that's where I stayed."

"What did your parents say about that? I know mine would have been ticked to lose their basement space."

"Dad doesn't care and mom was just happy to have me back under her roof. She worries. A lot. She didn't want me to try college in the first place. She has a lot of fears about the world and about me. She didn't think I could handle college or living on my own."

They were quiet as they waited for the stop light to turn green.

"And she was right. I couldn't handle it."

"I wouldn't say that. Maybe the circumstances weren't right for you at that time. Maybe the combination of moving away from home on top of college classes was too much. It is for many people - me included. At least, I think it would have been. Unlike you, I didn't even try. I lived with my folks while I attended college."

"Yeah? How'd that work for you?"

"About what you'd think. It was cheaper since I didn't have much money. It was nice to come home to a meal on the table, the house was clean and if I'd left my laundry in the hamper, it would be done, folded and put away."

"Does the term 'spoiled brat' come to mind?"

"Spoiled, maybe but not 'brat'. Never. Uh huh, not me."

"You didn't have a sister like Mel. She ruined that part for me. She harped and harped to our mother about independence and that mom was hampering me so much that mom finally stopped doing my laundry for me. Thanks, Mel. Couldn't she have picked on something else?"

"It sucks when you have to wash your own dirty underwear." Lori turned her head to look at Jeff. "What would your parents say if you told them you were moving out?"

"My dad wouldn't say much either way. Sometimes it's hard to be heard over mom, anyway. She'd blow a gasket." Jeff tilted his head toward Lori. "That was an idiom in case you didn't notice. It does spruce up the language and give you a visual of what my mother would do."

"Are they old and need you to look after them?"

"Not really. Well, they are old, but they're not infirm or anything. They can manage themselves pretty well. No, it's more that mom thinks she's looking after me. The more she can shelter me, the better a mother she thinks she is."

"Do you need to be sheltered?" Lori asked.

"There are some nice things about it. If someone else cooks, cleans and does the grocery shopping that leaves me more time for my coding. That's really taken a hit since I started at the bakery. I can't stay up all night working on coding and graphics projects anymore because Ellie's counting on me at the bakery. Before I started, she was close to losing the place, but with my deli cooking her lunch and supper crowd really picked up. She's given me two raises since I started, which is okay, but I used to make a nice pile of change with coding gigs. I still have some contracts I'm working on but it's harder to fit in the time now."

"Being a grown up sucks, sometimes."

"You know Lori, I think I like you. You come across all sweetness and light and uptightness but that's not really you. When you let your hair down, you're all right." He waited a beat. "Did you catch that idiom?"

CHAPTER 5

Before the kids arrived for the next Little Chef's session, Jeff entered the kitchen with his grocery bags. He fished something out of his pocket and told Lori to hold out her hand and close her eyes.

"What for?" she asked.

"You really aren't good at taking orders, are you?"

Lori saw herself as the most easy to get along with person ever. She worked with teachers in their rooms all day, every day, following their lead, fitting into their way of doing things. She thought compliance was her middle name. There was something about Jeff that brought out the rebel in her. That thought provoked a giggle. A rebel - it was soooo out of character for her. "What will happen if I do?" she asked Jeff.

"Just trust me, all right? Now, close your eyes and hold out your hand."

To prove she was no chicken, she complied. After all, what could he do? Put something squishy in her hand to try to scare her? Fat chance. Growing up with her neighbor, Jack, had cured her of going all girly over anything. That would have just encouraged Jack to torment her more.

Something light and spongy dropped in her hand. Lori opened her eyes. "What's this?"

"It's a glow-in-the-dark key chain. Can't have my number one Little Chef helper getting mugged in some dark parking lot because she can't find her keys."

Mel and Rita chatted in the hallway as they dropped their kids off for Little Chef's the next week. Steve entered the kitchen, announcing his presence with a "Hi."

Karen, the only other person in the room at the time, looked over her should at Steve then returned her gaze to the radishes she was washing. "Hi," she replied. Then she used one shoulder to hike her glasses into a higher position on her nose.

Steve moved over to the sink to see what she was doing. He washed his hands the way Jeff had taught them, then reached for some radishes, copying Karen's movements.

He looked sideways at Karen a couple times, then said, "Why do you wear such dorky glasses?"

In the hallway, Rita stiffened, outrage on her face. Mel waited to see what would happen.

"Because they're the only ones I have," said Karen.

"Oh." The kids continued cleaning the radishes.

In the hallway, Rita was outraged. She turned to Mel, "You heard that. How dare he speak to my daughter that way? Do you see the way she is bullied and mistreated in this school? What are you going to do about it?"

Mel pushed off from the wall she'd been leaning on and went to the kitchen doorway. "Karen, would you come here for a minute, please?" She returned to where Rita waited.

"Karen? You're calling out Karen? What about that boy who spoke that way to my daughter?"

"Hi, Karen," Mel said, "Come on into the washroom a minute with your mom and I, please."

In the girls' bathroom, Mel positioned Karen in front of the mirror in between the two women. "Karen, look in the mirror. Why do you think Steve asked that question about your glasses?"

Karen's eyes wandered at first then focused on her own face. She studied her reflection with curiosity. "Because they do look dorky?" Karen asked.

"What about them do you think is dorky?"

Beside them, Rita's breath came out in a short gasp. She started to interrupt but Mel held up her hand, motioning for her to wait.

Karen continued to study herself. "One side is higher than the other. I'd say it's about five-eighths of an inch higher. Or maybe the left side is five-eighths of an inch lower. Which do you think, mom?"

"Well, I, I, I'm not sure. I hadn't noticed," her mother said. Mel looked skeptically at Rita over Karen's head.

"Do you like the way your glasses look?" asked Mel.

"Not really. They are kind of dorky but I guess I'm used to them. They bug me when I'm reading and sometimes I get headaches. Dad said that probably because my glasses aren't right."

"Not right! When did he say that? This is the first I've heard about it."

Mel ignored Rita and continued to focus on Karen. "That must be uncomfortable. Is there anything you think you can do about it?"

Karen used her middle finger to push her glasses higher onto her nose. That helped a bit, but not enough. Her thumb and index finger grasped one sidearm and pushed it higher until the glasses were almost level under her eyebrows.

"How does that feel now?"

"Better."

Mel asked, "How does it *look* now?"

"Better." Karen smiled at herself in the mirror. "Less dorky." She turned her face to show her mother the new look. The movement put them out of whack again. Karen tried to straighten them again.

"What can you do about your glasses?" Mel persisted.

"I can keep pushing them right."

"Can you think of anything else you can do?"

Karen's middle finger returned to the bridge of her glasses. "Maybe if I held my hand like this..."

"Well, that is one idea but I was thinking of something a little more permanent. Is there anything your mom could do?"

Karen looked doubtful. She reached for her mother's hand and replaced her own finger with her mom's. "She could hold them for me, but she's not at school all the time."

Mel smiled. "What if you asked your mom to take you back to the optometrist's to have your glasses straightened? They could fix them so that neither of you has to hold them in position."

"Could we, mom?"

"Of course. I didn't know they were a problem or I would have suggested it myself. I've just gotten used to seeing them this way."

"Thanks, mom. I gotta get back to the kitchen. They need my help."

Left alone, Rita and Mel looked at each other in the mirror.

"God," Rita said. "How could I not have noticed? I look at Karen all day. We're close and hang out together. I'm pretty much her only friend. How could I look at her but not really see something as obvious as those crooked glasses?"

"Because you're human. If that's the worst parenting faux pas you ever make, count yourself lucky."

Rita still seemed stricken.

"Look. Karen's okay. *You* seem way more upset about it than she is. Even the thing with Steve didn't bother her."

"I almost forgot about what that boy said. Are you going to let him get away with that?"

"Get away with what? He asked her a question. She answered the question. In the kids' minds, that's all there was to it. Kids are honest; they say what they think. If they have a question, they ask it.

"I know you worry about your daughter being hurt. But Karen was all right. Steve wasn't being mean - he just asked a question. And, you gotta admit, her glasses were pretty crooked."

"I swear they weren't that bad when she left for school this morning. Wait. I know what happened. She whacked her head on the car door as she was getting out. I bet that twisted them even more."

"Probably," Mel agreed. "We've got almost an hour to kill while we wait for the kids. Want to go grab a coffee at the place down the street?"

CHAPTER 6

"You look like you've got a lot on your mind." Mel blew on her latte to cool it.

"I can't believe Tad didn't mention Karen's glasses to me."

"Maybe he forgot. My husband, Ben and I get busy and forget to tell each other things. Just ask him when you get home."

"Can't. He won't be there."

"Working?"

"Yeah, working. All the time he's working. He's a salesman," Rita explained. "He used to be away just a couple nights a week and was always home on weekends. Then with this economic down turn, he's had to travel farther and doesn't make it home at all on the week days."

"That's rough. He must get pretty tired of being away from home."

"He complains all the time that he's tired. Well, he used to complain to me but in the last months, we hardly talk. First it was that he didn't get back to his hotel until too late to call. Then, he was too tired to drive all the way home for just the weekend and stayed in the city. And then he said that the hotel bills were killing him so he took an apartment. He hasn't been home in five weeks."

"Karen must miss her dad."

"Less than I do. At least she's seen him. Twice, he's sent a ticket for her to take the train to spend the weekend with him."

"That must have been fun for her."

"Yes. He told her it was their special time. Karen never wondered why Tad sent just one ticket - one for Karen, but none for me."

"Oh."

"Yes, oh."

"Maybe you're reading more into this. It could be that he really is tired from his traveling. Have you asked him?"

Rita shook her head. "I'm afraid to. I'm afraid that if I ask him if we're now separated, he'll answer and then it will be true."

"Wouldn't you rather know the truth?"

"No! This way I still have the hope that it's temporary and we'll be back together again."

"Are you sure you're reading the situation right?"

"Oh, who knows?"

"Do you think part of it is that you have a child on the autism spectrum?"

"Could be," said Rita. "It has been hard. It's not like raising a typical child."

"I'm rather new to this parenting thing myself; I've only been married a year and Kyle's only been in his life for about a year more than that. Before that I was just a teacher who had these kids for six hours a day. Now I see it from the other side of the desk. It's different, isn't it?"

"Tell me about it. I don't think teachers get what it's like at home."

"And teachers say that parents don't know what it's like to have that one or two children with autism as part of a class of twenty-five."

"It's not easy for any of us, I guess," Rita admitted.

"If it's hard for us, how hard do you think it is for these kids? They sipped their lattes and thought about life from their kids' viewpoints.

"We used to be good together," Rita said. "Tad and I was the pair that you'd expect to stay together forever. We were so excited when we were expecting Karen. We thought we had so much to offer a child."

Mel nodded her understanding.

"At first we thought we had a precocious baby. She was so self-contained and easy to manage. Other parents complained about how demanding their baby was, but Karen could lay in her crib and stare at her mobile for literally hours. She met all her developmental milestones on time or early. She could amuse herself for hours. I even took classes and finished my degree when she was a toddler, she was so well-behaved. And talk - wow, her vocabulary astounded everyone who saw her."

"She seems like a very bright girl."

"Oh, she is."

"Is that holding her back?"

Rita bristled. "What do you mean? She's smart. That's the best thing about her."

"I'm sorry to hear that."

"What the hell do you mean?"

"Look, I'm not trying to be disrespectful. It's great that Karen is an intelligent child. But, and I'm thinking as a parent here, when there's something different about a kid and we know that that child finds life difficult and maybe creates some difficulties in school, we want the adults to focus on the positive - to see the best things about our kid. Karen's smart, so we want teachers to see those smarts. We find ways to have the child demonstrate her smarts and we insist on good marks."

Rita nodded. "Yes, we do. And Karen loves showing off her knowledge and her perfect report cards."

"Ah. That's the problem, isn't it?"

"That she's smarter than other kids?"

"No, that she demonstrates her smarts all the time."

"Are you trying to say that that's a bad thing? Being smart is good."

"Yeeees, but what if her smarts or demonstrating her smarts gets in the way of her social interactions?"

"Karen doesn't really care that much about kids or socializing. She hasn't exactly had good experiences with them"

"Why is that?"

"They haven't been nice to her. In fact, they've been mean."

"What does Karen do then?"

"Sometimes she cries, sometimes she talks over top of them and sometimes she gets mad."

"Is that working for her?"

"It's the other kids. They don't understand someone like Karen. Maybe they're jealous of her brain, at least that's what we tell her."

"Oh, dear." Mel was not known for her diplomacy but she picked up from Rita's face that she was coming on a bit strong. She gave a smile and tried a Dr. Phil voice. "How's that working for her?"

"She's had to be strong. We've told her to ignore the other kids."

Like a broken record, "And how's that working for her?"

Rita's shoulders dropped and she addressed her coffee cup. "We're trying but so far it's *not* working for her. She still gets hurt. And frustrated. She doesn't know why the kids don't like her."

"I know why."

"What?" Rita was affronted again.

"Sorry. That didn't come out quite right." Mel took a sip of coffee and gave herself a second to think. "I have seen how the kids respond to Karen and I think I understand where things break down for her."

Rita just waited.

"Look. Life is about give and take. Karen might have some great information to offer, but it's all one-sided. She talks on and on without giving anyone else a chance to speak."

"Yeah, she does that all right."

"If you on occasion find that annoying, how do you

think other children would feel? They just move on. There are other kids to play with, ones who will be interactive with them."

"I've seen that happen to her. Sometimes Karen will just keep on talking even if her audience moves away. She gets on a roll about what she wants to talk about."

"Well, that's a drag for other kids. The unwritten rule about interactions is that you talk a bit, and then I talk a bit. Typical kids watch their audience to see how they're coming across and if the other person is getting bored, they change the topic or ask a question or do something to draw the other person back in. Karen does not seem to have these skills."

"No, she doesn't, but that's part of having Asperger's."

"Is it?"

"Of course it is. If you knew anything about autism spectrum disorders, you'd know that."

"I like to think that I actually do know something about ASDs. My Master's degree was all about this. And I went back for that extra training because I was teaching so many kids with ASDs. That's been my job for almost fifteen years. And, now I'm mom to a little guy on the spectrum."

"ASDs?"

"That's the short form for autism spectrum disorders."

"Oh, right. Sorry, I didn't mean to imply that you don't know. It's just that I most often run into people who don't understand."

"Well, I do understand, at least about as well as anyone can who is not on the spectrum themselves. And yes, having weak Theory of Mind skills is common to people on the autism spectrum."

"Theory of Mind?"

"Toddlers and preschoolers, like people with autism spectrum disorders have weak Theory of Mind. They believe that the world revolves around them. As that toddler matures, he realizes that other people may have likes, dislikes, thoughts and intentions that differ from his. Then he gains skills at guessing what might be in that other person's mind, based on their facial expression and body language."

"That's typical kids, not those with autism or Asperger's."

"True, but kids on the spectrum can learn. Some of this might not come to them automatically, but they can gain some of these skills, becoming better and better at it."

"That obviously hasn't happened to Karen yet."

"I'm not sure how easy it is to develop those skills on her own, especially when she is not even aware that she's lacking something that came naturally to other kids. You can help her, though. She can definitely learn to get better at this."

"How?"

"What do you do at home when she talks on and on about

something?"

"This is an embarrassing, but I usually just tune her out. Karen doesn't seem to notice. Sometimes I even walk out of the room and I can still hear her carrying on as if I was still there."

"Sounds like she's more talking *at* you rather than *with* you."

"Definitely! It gets so tiring sometimes."

"I think the kids in her class would agree with you. And as they enter their teen years, my guess is that the kids will have even less patience with this."

Rita looked pained. "So, how can I help her?"

Mel thought a minute. "Here's something off the top of my head.

"Kids with ASDs are visual learners - they take in information that they see more easily than things that they hear."

"What if you made a picture of a red stop sign? Do you own a stop watch or egg timer?"

"Yes, we have a kitchen timer, I think."

"Maybe try setting it for say thirty seconds. Face Karen and let her talk freely about whatever she wants, until the timer goes. Explain that now it's your turn to talk and she must be quiet until the timer goes again. Hold up the stop sign as a visual reminder. Try to make what you say connected to whatever Karen was talking about. Keep going back and forth, taking turns.

"Once Karen has the knack of being quiet and letting you have your turn, add in some other aspects, things we do in general conversation."

"Like what?"

"Take your pick. One could be that Karen needs to make eye contact with you while she's talking, or while you're talking."

"Ha. She's often staring off into space while she talks."

"That's why she missing valuable information about how her partner is responding to her conversation. If she's not watching for the body language and facial expression, she'll have no idea that she's bored the other person."

"You think I could teach her things like that?"

"Definitely. Try standing in front of a mirror with her and demonstrating what a bored face looks like. Have Karen imitate your bored expression. You can carry on to other emotions as well. Is Karen kind of a techie kid? Does she like computers?"

"Definitely."

"Then there's a computer game she might like. You can get a free demo of Gaining Face at this website." Mel grabbed a napkin and wrote the url: http://www.stonemountainsoftware.com/GainingFace/index.html.

"Let's get back to what you were saying before - about this stop sign business."

"Right. Sorry, I got side-tracked. Okay, so by now Karen is used to the pattern of she talks then you talk, etc. But now you need to change it up. Whatever she says must be related to what you said during your turn. If that's too hard for her right off, then have her repeat the last sentence you said. This will force her to listen to you, rather than letting her mind dwell on her own stuff while you talk and she waits for her turn. She might find this difficult."

"Yes, she will. I don't think my little girl will be a happy camper."

"Is she a happy camper now?"

"Not really, at least not some of the time."

"Over time vary the turn-taking times because we don't always talk in just thirty second bursts. You can gradually eliminate the stop sign and then the timer as she learns the give and take of conversation."

"You think this will work?"

"I know it will. I've done this or something like it with other kids."

"If you're interested in this stuff, there's a website I like. It's called Do2Learn. It explains some of the social difficulties kids have and gives lots of suggestions on how to be helpful."

Rita shoved the napkin back at Mel so she could add the URL.

http://www.do2learn.com/SocialSkills/overview.htm

"Social skills, eh? Maybe Tad and I could use some of these."

"Couldn't we all, couldn't we all," agreed Mel. "I know a couple guys who are *not* on the spectrum who could use some brushing up."

"Thanks for listening about Tad and me. I wonder if I dare talk to him about some of this social skill stuff and Karen."

The last of the kids wrapped up slices of asparagus-caramelized-onion-feta quiche and separate packages of coconut meringue macaroons and then moved into the hallway. As they left the kitchen, Lori and Jeff leaned on the counter with their backs to the sink, chatting companionably. When the room was full of children, they had to stand fairly close to make room for everyone. Now that the kids cleared out, neither thought to move away.

"Isn't this a cozy little scene?" A harsh voice came from the door. A fellow in a well-used, oil-stained denim vest filled the doorway. "What's going on here?"

"Jack!" Lori sprang away from the sink and from Jeff. "What are you doing here?"

"I want to know what *you're* doing here."

"I'm working."

"Is this what you call 'work' these days?"

Jeff unfolded himself from his relaxed stance and took a step closer to Lori. "Do you know this guy, Lori?" If he'd been a cat, he would have puffed up his tail and ruff.

Nervousness was in Lori's voice. "Yeah. It's Jack. He's my, my..."

"Spit it out, Lori dearest. Can't you tell this dweeb that I'm your guy?"

"Jack, it's not like that and you know it," said Lori.

Jack advanced and grabbed Lori's arm in his tight fist. "I know no such thing. You're mine - always have been, always will be. Don't even try to forget that."

"Jack, I haven't seen you in months."

"I've had things to do. And right now I have things to do - *we* have things to do so your little 'work' is over for the day. Let's go." He gave a less than gentle tug on Lori's arm.

Taking another step closer, Jeff asked, "Lori, do you want to go with this guy?"

"It's okay, Jeff. Jack and I go way back."

"I don't care about the way back part. Do you want to go with him now?"

Jack looked between Lori and Jeff. "What gives with you two? Little Lori, have you been stepping out on me?"

Looking more at Jeff than Jack, Lori replied, "It's not like that between us and you know it, Jack." To Jeff, she said, "We grew up together. We were neighbors."

Jack laughed. "Right. We were much more than that."

Lori's look at Jeff pleaded with him to believe her.

Jack backed out of the kitchen, pulling Lori with him. "Get your sweet ass in motion, little Lori. I have plans for you tonight."

"Lori?" Jeff's voice asked his question. "Do you want to go with him?"

Lori half turned as Jack marched her down the corridor. "It's okay. I'm fine. Jack needs me. I'll see you next week."

Jack agreed with some of that. "I need your car, that's for sure. But as for seeing him next week, well, we'll see about that."

As they neared the outside door, it opened and Mel's husband Ben came into the hall. His face darkened when he saw Jack and his grip on Lori. "Hey! Lori, what's going on here? Is this guy bothering you again?"

"This place is a regular little Lori defense team. I'm not hurting Lori, so back off." The sneer was back in Jack's voice.

Ben planted himself in the middle of the doorway. "Lori? Are you all right? Do you need help?"

"Please, it's fine. I'm fine. Just leave us alone. Jack and I are leaving now."

"You got that right," echoed Jack.

"Are you sure, Lori?" Jeff asked as he came up beside Ben. "You don't have to go with him if you don't want to."

"I'm fine, really, guys." Lori's eyes and voice and body language all made a liar of her words. "Look, just leave us alone. We're going. See you next week." They went out into the dark night.

Ben looked at Jeff, who looked even less happy than Ben. Jeff pushed open the door and went into the parking lot. Ben followed. Together, they watched Lori dig through her purse while Jack drummed his fingers on the roof of the car, griping all the while. When the glow-in-the-dark key chain came into sight Jack snatched it from Lori's hand and got behind the wheel of the car.

Jeff called, "Need a ride, Lori?"

But she was already rounding the front of the car and pulling open the passenger door. She was hardly in her seat when the car took off out of the parking lot, tires squealing.

"Do you think she's all right?" Jeff asked.

"Probably, but I'm not sure. I saw that guy with her once last year. I didn't like the way he treated her then and it was no better now. Mel lectures me about respecting the choices people make even when you don't agree, but I don't know about this."

"There's something else I didn't know."

"What?"

"I didn't know you could make an exit like that with an old Corolla."

Ben grinned.

Jeff asked his brother-in-law, "What brings you here tonight?"

"Mel. She texted me that she's at the coffee shop with Karen's mother and they lost track of time. She asked if I'd stop by just in case they're a couple minutes late and hold on to Kyle and Karen until they get her. The kids are waiting in my car."

"What were Mel and Rita talking about that they forgot the time? Mother's aren't supposed to do that. They must have been going hard at it."

"Do you think that bodes well for you and me?"

"As Mel tells me, 'It's not always about you'. Do you have a guilty conscience about something?"

"I'm pretty sure my dirty socks from yesterday are somewhere under the bed."

"Then let's hope that you're the only one in trouble tonight. I don't want to think about what kind of trouble Lori could be in with that guy."

CHAPTER 7

Gloria Stewart raised her cheeks from her hands. Here they come again, she thought. The first bell rang and she could hear the voices and tromping of the kids as they came down the hallway. Soon, the grade six students would enter her classroom, disrupting her peace. How many more months until she could leave this place for good? She took a quick look at her register to remind herself. "I can do this," she said under her breath.

There was Karen's voice, overriding the others. As Karen cleared the doorframe, her conversation continued. Gloria wasn't sure it could be classed as a conversation since no one appeared to be talking with her. Or listening to her.

Karen spied the teacher and Gloria's heart sank. Karen came up to her and continued to talk as if Gloria had been her target audience all along. Whatever was the child saying? Something about that Little Chef's club and chateaubriand? Who cares, she thought. Even if she knew what chateaubriand was for sure, Gloria was positive it was beyond her present budget. Her attention drifted back to Karen; the child was still going on and on. How did her parents stand it?

She raised her voice. "Take your seats, please class." Karen continued, uninterrupted. Looking pointedly at the student, Gloria said even louder, "Karen, that means you. Go sit down now."

Karen looked a little startled, but complied. She really wasn't a bad child, Gloria thought, just talkative. What was that saying of her grandmother's? Something about talking the hind leg off a mule? Who knew what it meant, but it did fit Karen. No wonder the kids avoided her. But at least Karen wasn't outwardly defiant like some of the other students.

The morning wore on. As she lectured then assigned seat work, Gloria's mind wandered back to those days when she first started teaching thirty some years ago. Back then, kids were to sit with hands folded on their desks. They did not speak without being asked and certainly never without first raising their hands. There was none of this calling out or chatting with a neighbor. Nowadays, the principal informed her that group work was encouraged; kids were to discover things rather than have facts told to them by the teacher. Discussions, rather than straight telling were supposedly the way to go. Wasn't it more efficient for a trained professional to stand at the front of the room and lecture? Wouldn't learning happen better in a silent room? But no, silence was a precious commodity in the current classroom.

Social studies period was coming up in a minute. Gloria braced herself for this was a subject where she tried to do as she was instructed. She'd planned for a discussion on the purpose of national parks.

Well, this was not going well. The discussion derailed the minute Karen started talking. She treated the class to every minute detail of her family's trip to Yellowstone - every excruciating detail, including where they stopped for bathroom breaks. That part got a laugh from the class. Although Gloria herself was ready for some comic relief, getting the kids back into listening mode was a chore in itself. Saying sharply, "Karen. Karen!" Ah, that worked, at least momentarily. All the subtle things she'd already tried had had no effect. Saying that someone else needed a turn, that's enough, we're moving on and any other clues had not stopped Karen's monologue. Karen even seemed oblivious to the shuffling in the seats, the fact that no one looked at her, nor the teacher's back as she wrote on the board. That child simply would not stop talking. Pity. Some of what she had to say might have been interesting if it came out in smaller doses.

Oh, dear. Her mind drifted for just those few seconds, and Karen started up again.

"And then...," Karen began.

"Enough! Karen, someone else needs a turn now."

"...we went to...".

"Karen! Stop talking. We're moving on now." Gloria's voice was sharper than intended, but how did you get that child to quit talking?

"Yeah, Karen, shut up will ya?" one of the boys said.

Snickers and "Yeah" and "Finally" came from various corners of the room.

Karen looked around, noticing that everyone was looking at her and laughing or smirking. She slouched in her seat. What had she done wrong this time? She was on topic and she was telling them some really neat stuff about Yellowstone National Park. A tear formed at the corner of her eye. These kids were so mean. And stupid. She probably knew more about Yellowstone than all of them put together. Didn't they want to learn? Why were they always so mean? Her arms crossed and she slouched further in her seat.

His key jiggled the faulty lock until it opened. A stale smell wafted out the door and Tad was greeted by darkness. No aroma of a home-cooked meal. No welcoming lights. No smiling face to greet him with a hug and a kiss.

This was life on the road. Well, maybe not quite. Life on the road used to consist of an endless supply of hotel rooms, whose decor all ran together in his mind. Then the hours of driving home in the dark for a quick visit with his wife and daughter, then an early morning rise to get back on the road again.

He had thought that using an apartment as a home base would make this life better. At least it was the same bed he slept in much the time recently, but it wasn't the same. He missed the mattress Rita had spent so much time selecting and the soft, Egyptian cotton sheets she insisted were so much better. At the time he had not given it much thought, but she was right. Those sheets beat the rough cotton-polyester mix he was using now.

It was eight o'clock at night. He just got in. There was little in the fridge other than condiments, a case of beer and questionable fuzzy growths. The cupboards yielded a box of cereal, some crackers and a package of rigatoni noodles. Not even any pasta sauce. A beer would do while he faced the thought of yet another meal brought by the pizza delivery guy.

This was not how Tad had imagined his forties would play out. Huh, play. When was the last time he had time to play?

As her car squealed out of the school's parking lot, Lori scrambled to fasten her seat belt. "Easy on the tires, Jack," she said. "They're just new."

"All the more rubber for us to peel."

"Can you slow down a bit? Where are we going?"

"I need some wheels and a place to stay. But first, you're going to buy me a burger. I haven't eaten all day."

"There's a fast food place if you turn left at the next light."

Jack turned on the yellow light, not making it through the intersection before the signal turned red. Lori grabbed the door handle as Jack turned sharply into the drive through lane of the restaurant.

"Are you *that* hungry? Did you have to drive so fast?"

"Don't rag on me, Lori babe. I'm hungry and it's been a long day." He ordered through the microphone, cocking his head at Lori when the disembodied voice asked if they wanted anything else. Lori shook her head, no. "That's right. You and that pansy lover boy already ate. I could smell it in the hallway of that school." The voice stated the price for the food and Jack held out his hand to Lori. "Cough it up, babe. I'm flat broke."

With a sign, Lori rummaged in her purse for her wallet and came up with a twenty dollar bill. She bit her lip as Jack paid, pocketing the change.

"Where do you live, little Lori?" Jack drove with his burger in one hand, his extra-large soft drink between his knees and the box of French fries in the cup holder.

Lori started to give him directions then asked, "Why do you want to go there? Drive to your hotel or wherever you're staying and I'll drop you there then go home."

"I'm going where you're going. I told you I need a place to stay and your pad is it."

"But my place is tiny - just a one bedroom with a futon couch. It's too small for you."

"Then I guess that's where you'll sleep. Or, we could share your bed - your choice."

Lori gave him a withering look, trying to mask her distaste. "Jack you can't just drop in here and expect me to put you up. I like my privacy."

"Little Lori, you owe me and don't you forget it. I saved your pretty little ass more than once so if now and then you need to save mine, it's only fair. Right?"

Lori cringed. She did owe him. But how much? Would this debt never be over?

Maybe a normal conversation would help. "What have you been doing with yourself, Jack?"

"Are you being polite or do you really want to know, Little Lori? I've had a few deals go bad and need a place to hide out for a while."

"How long's a while? And what do you mean by 'hide out'?"

"About what you'd think. And I'll stay until I have a plan."

"I could help you with that."

"Ah, Little Lori, you have not a clue how to make a plan that would work in my life."

"Jack, you can't keep living this way and you can't stay at my place."

As subdued Lori entered Gloria's classroom. She was exhausted from sleeping on her lumpy futon and trying to sleep over Jack's snores resounding from her bedroom.

This was her scheduled period to help in the grade six room. She took in the teacher's exasperated look directed at Karen, then at Karen slumped in her desk. Ordinarily Lori would head right over to Karen but today she just didn't have it in her to tackle yet another problem. She'd wait a minute to see what was going on before jumping in.

From his desk near the window, Steve said, "We went to Yellowstone once too. It was neat. We saw some of the same things Karen did."

Karen's head perked up and she turned to Steve. Oh no, Gloria thought. Here we go again and I just got her shut down. She looked over at Lori, nodded and gestured to the front of the room, the cue to take over.

Lori put up her hand, her signal for silence with the kids. "So, two of you have been to Yellowstone. Anyone else?"

Two others raised their hands. "Great. Let's take turns. Think about one and just one thing you did or saw at Yellowstone that you'd like to share with the class. Steve, you go first, please."

"My dad and I hiked the Osprey Falls Trail. My mom had to stay back with my little sister because she wasn't big enough. You have to be strong and it took us all day. It was a hard walk and my dad was puffing. I held his hand at the steepest places 'cuz he said he needed my help. At the bottom there's this neat waterfall. We didn't see any bears, though."

"Thanks, Steve. Now Karen, what is the *one* thing you want to tell us about?"

"You've probably heard about Old Faithful, the most famous geyser in the world, but I liked Castle Geyser better. It erupts twice a day and is the noisiest. It takes about fifteen minutes to warm up, then it's roaring like a steam train and erupts with bursts that rise eighty feet in the air."

Lori quickly interjected. "Interesting, Karen. Now it's Peter's turn."

"We didn't see bears either, but we watched a family of otters play at Trout Lake. It's a really steep walk and I had to help my mom on the way down. From the lake you walk to a creek and there are these trout swimming upstream and jumping out of the water."

Karen looked like she wanted to add a story, but Lori's eyes found Karen's, she gave a slight shake of her head and angled her body away from Karen. Lori pointed a finger at the next child, smiled and nodded for Joan to speak.

After Joan's turn, Lori addressed the class. "Interesting stories. Now we get to ask these people questions about their trips. But there's a catch. Yesterday you were working with Mrs. Stewart on writing sentences. This time I want you to speak a sentence - just one.

"Think about what these people have told you about Yellowstone and ask a *one* sentence question to one of them." She addressed the four who had told their tales. "Your job is to answer the question in *one* sentence. Got it?"

"But what if one sentence isn't enough? There's a lot to tell about geysers." Karen was not happy with this limitation.

"One sentence. And, your sentence must answer the question you're asked. No adding other information. Think hard about the question you're given and answer only that question. This is part of the conversation skills we've been working on."

Gloria sat back and listened. When she first learned that there would be an EA in her room some of the time, she'd not had a clue. Back when she'd been teaching full-time, there were no such things as Educational Assistants - you were on your own with the kids. She'd opposed the idea of having another adult in her room, but the principal, Dr. Hitkins, insisted.

It was okay. Lori actually helped, plus she gave Gloria a break when it was becoming too much. That's the reasons Dr. Hitkins gave for having an EA, but whatever works.

And Lori was certainly useful at keeping that Karen child under control. Not that Karen acted up, but lord, how that child could talk. Any provocation and she'd be off, expounding on something or other. She was smart, yes - super smart obviously, but if she'd only shut sometimes up you could stand listening to what she had to say.

Dr. Hitkins had warned her about Karen - something about a syndrome called Asperger's. Well, Karen looked all right to her, it was just her incessant lecturing that got on her nerves. And not just on the teacher's nerves. Gloria saw the students roll their eyes when Karen got going. She'd see Karen go up to some kid and for a few minutes things might go all right, then Karen would go on and on and on about something to do with cooking and the other kid would walk away. Karen might trail behind, still talking or sometimes stand there talking to herself. It was unnatural.

But Lori had managed this discussion well, allowing Karen to talk but in limited amounts. In this controlled situation, the kids actually addressed Karen and listened to her. Even though Karen was an annoying child, Gloria felt a bit sorry for her. She was doomed to a lonely life.

Jeff had chateaubriand on his mind. Karen had infected him.

"Ellie," he asked, "do you think your customers would appreciate a fine piece of chateaubriand with Bercy sauce?"

"Probably, if they had a clue what it was. I have no idea what you're talking about."

Jeff explained the intricacies of cooking such a fine slab of meat.

"Whoa. Just how fine are we talking?"

When Jeff explained about the pricey cut, Ellie kyboshed the idea. "There's no way my customers are going to pay enough for a chateaubriand sandwich for me to recoup my costs." She thought some more. "But what if we had a special dinner one night, something we advertised well ahead of time. We could have live music and make it an upscale experience."

They both thought about the implications. Ellie asked, "What else would you serve with the meal?" Then she wished she had not asked as Jeff waxed on about the possibilities. Ellie had learned to trust Jeff's food instincts so she didn't need all the details. "Just work it out. Come up with what you think of the best meal combo then give me a budget of projected costs and possibly revenue. We'll see if we can make this work."

This was what Jeff lived for - well this and computer coding. But when he was in the kitchen, creating divine menus was his forte.

Usually Jeff hyper-focused. He would get in his zone, tune out the rest of the world and concentrate. But today, his mind kept slipping. Thoughts of Lori and how she was with Jack last night intruded. Although he and Lori might not have hit it off well the first night of Little Chef, they'd worked together well since then. Some people might even call them friends, Jeff thought. He liked her, liked the way she was with the kids and the way she was with him. But that Lori disappeared the moment Jack had entered the kitchen last night.

Were they dating? Lori didn't act as if she liked the guy much, although she hadn't objected to going with him. Jack needed to learn some social skills; he hadn't treated Lori nicely, nor had he shown the proper social niceties to Jeff or to Ben. Maybe no one had taught him or maybe he was just rude.

Jeff hadn't liked the way Jack grabbed Lori's arm. Had she looked scared? Jeff wasn't that great with facial expressions, but Lori's mannerisms definitely changed once Jack showed up. He hoped she was all right.

Mel told him to run stuff by someone he trusted when he wasn't sure. He looked over at Ellie. He trusted her.

"El, something happened last night that I'm not sure about." When he had her attention, he continued. "After Little Chef's Lori and I were just talking when this guy came in. He looked rough to me, but Lori knew him. He grabbed Lori's arm and told her to come with him. Lori didn't look excited about seeing him."

"Did you ask her if she was all right?"

"Yeah. Several times, but she said she was okay. Then Ben came by and he asked the same questions. Lori went with the guy and gave him her car keys. They drove off, but I didn't have a good feeling about this guy. Lori didn't smile once after he arrived."

"Did she make it home in one piece?"

Jeff tilted his head to one side and looked at Ellie. "How could I know that?"

"Why don't you phone the school and see if she's there today?"

Jeff took out his phone, looked up the number and dialed. When his call was answered, he said, "Is Lori Nabaker there?"

The secretary said, "Yes, just a minute please.

Jeff hung up. "Yeah," he told Ellie. "They say she's there."

"Jeff, did you just do what I think you did?"

"Do you know how much sense that question *doesn't* make?" Jeff returned to his corned beef marinade.

CHAPTER 8

Gloria thought more about Karen as she made a cup of tea in her kitchen. If none of the kids could stand her, Karen's life would end up as lonely as Gloria's was right now.

She looked around the kitchen she'd shared with her husband of forty-two years. Two thirds of her life had been spent with him. Now, he was gone.

He'd been eaten alive from the inside out as the cancer progressed. A strong guy, he'd fought and fought, lingering far longer than expected. She knew he'd hung on for her, knew how lost she'd be without him.

While she loved him even more for that, the long, long illness nearly depleted all their savings. There was nothing left and her pension would not start for another two years. The mortgage on their house would be paid off in nine more months, thank goodness. And hard as it was to go back to teaching at age sixty-three, this one year contract was a godsend. She'd quit in June when the final mortgage payment came due. Her needs were small; she could survive on what remained of their tiny nest egg until her pension kicked in when she turned sixty-five. But for now, she had to get through this year of teaching.

At least it got her out of this silent house. Before the contract came up, she'd wander room to room, carrying her cup of tea, straightening pictures, inspecting for dust. There really wasn't much to looking after a house when only one person lived there. No more drywall dust to clean up after Jed tracked it in after work.

He'd loved his job as an independent contractor, doing jobs alone or with a tiny crew he called on from time to time. Independent work gave him freedom and he worked hard. But independent work gave him no pension, no insurance, no security. When he stopped work, the money stopped. They'd been frugal and saved some of what Gloria had earned all those years ago when she taught full-time. But as Jed picked up more and more work, he'd needed her help with the bookkeeping end of things and she'd given up her teaching job. Their lives had been so full, she'd not missed being in the classroom.

But after Jed died and all the bills and medical expenses rolled in, Gloria realized just what a mess she was in. The past year, attending to Jed's needs, watching him wither away, then holding his parchment skinned hand as he passed away had been a blur. She'd paid the utility bills as they came in, but paid little heed to their finances.

In retrospect, she would not have done anything differently. They'd had a good life together and Jed had loved his work, even if it didn't provide for their old age. Who would have thought they'd ever even get old?

Reality forced Gloria to look back at the teaching field and luckily a temporary position was available. But these kids! They were not like the children she taught thirty years ago. The young teachers seemed to take it in stride and roll with the new way of doing things. Even Lori, not even a trained teacher, handled the class better than she did. Maybe it was not just a different generation. Maybe she was simply old and tired.

Normally, Lori loved her little apartment. It was her haven, her safe place, something hers alone. After moving out of her parents' house, she'd shared with various girlfriends for years, but now could afford rent on her own. Only two rooms really, but hers.

The bedroom closet door could not open fully because of the queen size bed, but that was okay. She was nimble enough to hop over the end of the bed to lean into the closet.

The two person kitchen table sat beside the television, which perched on the corner of the one-walled galley kitchen's counter, facing the futon. Two halves of an old bi-fold door balanced on layers of concrete blocks, creating an overflowing bookshelf. A battered leather recliner took up one corner, a relic from her parents' basement. Leaning over the chair was a gorgeous floor lamp Lori had spied one day. Why would anyone put such a thing out with their garbage? Enchanted with the faceted glass of the shade, Lori had walked up to the house and knocked on the door. Surely, it was a mistake that such a thing of beauty was with the trash. No, the woman who answered the door assured her, they had not made a mistake. The lamp was junk. It didn't work, but she was welcome to it. The woman shut the door, shaking her head, muttering about this idiot young lady.

Lori had carted the thing the seven blocks home, cradling the shade in her hands. After painstakingly cleaning and polishing until the glass glistened, Lori found that the woman was quite right; it didn't work. But that's what the internet was for, right? It took two days to figure out the problem and gather the wiring materials, but now it was the pride of her home. It's glow perfectly set off the abundance of green and flowering plants lining her walls and adorning sturdy cardboard boxes covered with shawls and scarves.

But tonight, well tonight was different. As soon as she stepped over the threshold, she could smell the difference, the intrusion. Instead of the aroma created by greenery, she smelled what? Was that stale beer, sweat, pizza?

Please, don't let him still be here. But the sound of water running in the shower dashed her hopes. Jack. He had not left as she'd hoped. Well, at least he was showering.

Her gaze took in the shape of her sanctuary. While not a neat freak, Lori liked leaving her place reasonably orderly so she could come home and sink into the comfort of her space. Now, a grungy vest covered the arm of the chair, a pair of jeans partially covered the stained coffee cup, ashtray and pizza carton on the table. And, was that a pair of briefs hanging off her cherished lamp? Beside the chair was her favorite ficus, the one she'd trained and fertilized since she was fourteen. It now lay on its side, a few leaves separated from their stem, one broken branch oozing sap onto the polished hardwood and the flea market vase broken with a deep v-shaped chunk out of it.

The shower shut off and Jack emerged wearing only a towel - one of *her* towels. She rounded on him.

"Hey, Little Lori. What's for supper?"

"You creep! What have you done to my place? And what are you doing here? I want you gone."

"Don't get your panties in a wad. I told you I needed a place to crash for a while."

"Crash is right. You trashed my apartment as well. Just look at this place. Out. Out, out out! Get out of my place and out of my life."

"Is that any way to talk to your old buddy? After all I've done for you, you owe me, don't forget." He sauntered over to the chair and lamp, one hand reaching for the gotch decorating her favorite lamp, the other letting go of the towel.

"No," Lori yelled.

"What?" Jack asked as he stopped his dressing to turn towards her, Lori whipped around, facing the door she'd just come.

"Geez. Can't you at least get dressed in the bathroom?" she complained.

"My clothes were here." He pulled on his pants. "Now, what are you making for supper? I'm looking forward to a home cooked meal."

Lori's shoulders rose then fell. Breath hissed out her mouth. Her mouth opened but no intelligible words escaped. She whirled around, headed back into the hallway, slamming her door behind her. She leaned back against the wall, letting out her breath. Her fingers clenched again as she heard Jack call, "At least bring back some take-out if you're not going to cook."

Lori didn't care who heard her footsteps slamming down the stairs. The outside door tore against its hinges as she yanked it open then stormed down the street.

At first she was too mad to care where she walked - her feet took her wherever they pointed, as her mind churned.

Her stomach rumbled. The approaching darkness penetrated her consciousness and Lori realized that she should not spend the evening walking the streets. When she reached the next intersection and could read the street signs, she got her bearings. Just a couple blocks ahead was the bakery, run by Mel's sister-in-law, Ellie. And, it was the place where Jeff worked.

The lights of the bakery represented safety. The aromas spread welcoming cheer. The small place had a couple tables open.

From behind the counter, Ellie called a greeting. She and Lori had met a number of times. When Jeff heard Lori's name, he popped his head around the corner of the kitchen to check.

"You look cold," said Ellie. "What kind of warm-up drink do you fancy?"

While Lori sipped her chai tea, she and Ellie discussed the meal options on the chalkboard. "Really," Ellie said, "I'd recommend anything Jeff makes and he created everything listed there." The smell of the roasted corned beef was in the air and when Ellie said the harvest rye bread was baked that afternoon, Lori decided on the corned beef on rye with stone ground wine mustard and sauerkraut on the side. The homemade goodness seeped into her pores on the first bite. Delectable.

Once most of the supper crowd was served, Jeff had time to sit with Lori. He arrived carrying his cappuccino.

Jeff was not big on small talk, didn't see the point in it. "What's wrong?" he asked.

"Nothing. Everything's fine."

"Liar."

Lori raised one eyebrow and the side of her mouth crinkled up. Her eyes left Jeff's. She angled her body to take in more of the room.

Jeff did not take the hint. "Does this have anything to do with that guy who took you from Little Chef's?"

She looked pointed at him. "Some things are none of your business."

"You need a friend. I can be a friend." Then, he added, "Not just your Little Chef boss."

His smirk broke the ice and Lori leaned forward. Why not, she thought.

She could use an outside opinion.

"I came home from work today and Jack was in my apartment. Still. I told him he couldn't stay with me last night, but he did anyway. He took my bed and *I* slept on the futon. My lumpy futon. I told him he had to be gone before I got home from school. I unlock my door and there he is. Still. And my place was a mess." She shook her head at the vision of her neat little apartment contaminated by Jack and his mess. "Then, he expected me to cook for him."

"What is this guy to you?"

"Nothing."

"Right." Jeff's expression showed his skepticism.

"Well, we're friends. Sort of, or at least we were when we were kids. He grew up two houses down from us. We played together as little kids, then we drifted into boy things or girl things as we became teenagers and hardly saw each other except to wave if we passed the other going into our houses."

"Why does the guy act like he owns you?"

Lori stirred her chai more than it needed. "I do owe him." She sighed, debating whether or not to tell the rest of the story. Why not? Maybe an impartial viewpoint would help. Once when I was sixteen, I got into some trouble. There was this guy. He was pretty cool, or so I thought, but he never noticed me until one day. I was walking home from the library when he drove by. He stopped and asked if I wanted a ride. I was thrilled and got in. I started to give him directions to my house but he laughed and said we didn't need to go there. He drove to the edge of a park. There were street lights around but he parked in the corner of the lot that was darkest. There were a couple other cars but they were farther away."

Jeff thought he could see what was coming.

Lori said, "I never saw it coming. I thought he wanted to talk to me. That wasn't what he had in mind. At first he just slid closer and put his arm around my shoulders. Then he kissed me, gently at first. I didn't really mind although I was a bit uneasy. I wasn't experienced at all. Now I know that I should have listened to that feeling inside that something wasn't right, but I was so naive and I was flattered that he wanted me."

"What happened then? Did he..., were you...?"

"No. He'd hit the lock so my passenger door wouldn't open. We struggled, but he was so strong and I was so scared. My elbow hit the horn and it blasted. He pulled my arm away but I got it there again and kept sounding the horn as much as I could."

"Did that back him off?"

"He hit me. On the side of the head. I guess I was kind of stunned for a few minutes because I came to and my shirt was off and there was this guy pounding on the driver's side window. I opened my eyes to see what was going on and it was Jack. Then Jack saw me and yelled my name. Then he was gone."

"Shit. That creep just left you there. Figures."

"No, no, he didn't. He ran back carrying the tire iron from the trunk of his car. He was parked on the other side of the lot. He broke the side window, reached in and unlocked the door. He dragged Stan out of the car, threw him on the ground and kicked him in the head, then between his legs. He was breathing hard when he opened the passenger door and lifted me out."

"Were you okay?"

"Yeah. Just scared. Nothing too much happened other than the hit to my head. Jack pulled off his shirt and put it around me. Then he carried me to his car where his girlfriend waited. He told her to get in the backseat and put me in the front. He wanted to take me to the hospital but I wouldn't let him. I didn't want my parents to know how stupid I'd been."

"Couldn't they tell by looking at you that something was wrong?"

Lori shook her head. "They took me to his girlfriend's house and I stayed there. Jack made her phone my parents, pretending to be a friend from school. She said we'd run into each other at the library then went to her house to work on an assignment. It was getting late and we were still working, so she told them her parents said it was okay for me to stay there overnight. The next morning Jack picked me up, took me shopping for a new sweater that looked a bit like my ruined one, then took me home. He stayed talking with my parents so I got escape to the bathroom for a shower. By the time I dried my hair and had a nap, my parents had both left the house, so I had time to get my act together before they got home."

"Did you tell them later?"

"No. They never knew."

"Why didn't Jack tell?"

"He had enough in his past that he understood keeping things from your family. Things didn't turn out so well for him in his teen years. He dropped out of school, tried his hand at mechanics for a while, but there was more money to be made peddling. He had a couple close shaves with the police, and then got caught. He didn't have much on him so he only got two years less a day."

"Some nice friends you have."

"He was a nice guy. He saved me when he could have ignored the screams. He didn't even know it was me and he went to help a stranger. And, he never told my parents on me. I owe him for that."

"How many years ago was that?"

Lori thought for a second. "A little over eight."

"Have you never had an opportunity to repay him yet?"

"Oh, yes. He stops by every once in a while when he's in trouble. Like now. Sometimes he needs money; sometimes a place to stay. A couple times he needed to borrow a car."

"Do you get your car back?"

She hesitated. "Mostly. One time I didn't. He smashed it."

Jeff looked disgusted. "So this guy comes to your rescue one time when you were just a kid, then says you owe him. Over and over. How long do you think you're going to keep bailing him out of trouble?"

"I don't know. Forever I think Jack would say." A look of distaste crossed her face. She put her chin in her hands. "I'd be happy if I never saw him again. How's that for gratitude?"

"Reasonable. This guy can't just drop in and out of your life and expect you to put him up or give him money. What kind of trouble do you think he could be bringing to your door? If he's hiding out at your place, what sort of people do you think are after him? Do *you* want to get caught in the crossfire?" He grinned at Lori. "That's an idiom, you know."

That made Lori smile, the first real smile since she'd entered the bakery.

"Now what?" Jeff asked.

CHAPTER 9

He really should go hang up his suit jacket or it would be a wreck tomorrow. Instead, Tad pulled his tie from around his neck and threw it towards the offending jacket. Who cared if his clothes looked like he'd slept in them? It wasn't as if being impeccably dressed had bolstered sales these past months.

He settled farther into the saggy couch that came with his furnished apartment. The first week there, the smell had so offended him that he'd avoided the sofa. Now, it fit the rest of his life, so he used it.

Ahead of him a nineteen inch television showed players on a baseball field. The sound was off and Tad had no idea who was playing. He didn't care.

There seemed to be less and less he cared about. Except for Karen. Karen topped his list of things to care about. She was the reason why he kept on with this stupid job, determined to provide a good life for her.

But was he? The last time Karen was here she couldn't understand why he didn't come home anymore on weekends. His explanation that it was too far to drive didn't fly with her. She was too smart. She recited all the other times he had driven home. She was right.

Then he tried explaining that he worked weekends now. Karen just looked at him with those piercing eyes and for once, didn't speak. She was far, far too smart.

Tad remembered those early years with Karen, the years when they had been a true family. Karen was the most angelic baby, quiet, amusing herself for hours. She didn't scream to be held the way some kids did. She was content with herself. Rita and he took that to mean that already Karen was more mature than other babies. Then when she began talking - wow. She blew them and everyone who heard her out of the water. All that reading they'd done with her paid off. Suddenly she could recite those books word for word. She used the words in the proper context and her memory was prodigious.

As an only child, she had the undivided attention of her doting parents. She was an angel lining her books up by the hour, then switching to flipping through the pages over and over. The only times life became rough were when they changed things. Once Rita rearranged the living room furniture to accommodate their new, big screen television. You'd think the world had come to an end. They'd quickly put things back as best they could, even though their old, smaller TV was now gone. That was all their fault, of course. With a child as intelligent as Karen, they really should have included her in their plans, letting her know of the new living room arrangements. They reasoned that the problem was the cooking shows Karen was positively hooked on. Watching their television being carted out the door, she probably thought she'd never get to see her beloved shows again. They should have warned her that she could still watch them on the new set.

Other than that, she was easy to live with. Well, there was the clothes things but they learned to get around that. It seemed that while Karen loved purple, she hated the color orange and pitched an ungodly fit if someone wanted her to wear clothing that had orange in it. Still, that was easy to fix. Orange was overrated in clothes anyway and anyone could live without ever wearing orange. Hell, he didn't know if he'd ever in his life put on anything orange. It was lucky that they didn't live in the part of the country that required winter boots and heavy parkas because Karen detested the change of seasons that necessitated outerwear. Just donning a light jacket in winter was fight enough for then. But then, who in their right mind would want to live where there was snow anyway?

Theirs was a happily-ever-after story if ever there was one. The three of them made the perfect family. Until Karen started school.

They'd seen no need of preschool - that was for those kids who needed a helping hand to get ready for school. Karen aced all those readiness skills already. In fact, they had seriously discussed if it would be wiser to skip kindergarten altogether and start her in grade one. But a conversation with the school squelched that; they would not even entertain the idea. Resigned, he and Rita had vowed to make their home as enriching as possible for their brilliant child.

Then came kindergarten and all their lives changed. Karen, their confident, precocious little girl turned into a whiny, miserable hellion. She attacked her fellow students, sometimes indiscriminately, it seemed. Of course, she was just defending herself from the meanness of those other little creatures. She was so far ahead of them in all things academic that they were jealous.

The calls from the school started and the meetings. They seemed to think something was wrong with his darling. Huh! They just didn't know how to handle a child as smart as his Karen.

But the school insisted. They invited him and Rita to come observe at school. He didn't, of course. His job was much too demanding. Besides, shouldn't these teachers know how to do their own jobs?

Rita went. Over and over again and she became more subdued. When she tried to talk to Tad about it, to say that Karen did seem different than the other five year olds, he'd get mad. Of course she was different. She had an IQ thirty points above the other poor schmucks they put in her class. Those kids probably didn't understand half the words that came out of Karen's mouth. He had his doubts that some of those teachers even did.

Rita stopped trying to talk to him about it, but she'd sit on the couch and watch Karen play and talk to herself. Sometimes Rita would interrupt Karen and try to get her to talk about something Rita wanted to discuss. Karen resisted. Well, who wouldn't? A kid that bright had her own agenda. She was a strong-willed kid and happy with herself. He got bugged too when he was engrossed in something and Rita kept interrupting him.

Then came the permission forms. The school wanted to test his daughter. It was about time. Surely now they recognized that they had a little genius on their hands. So, he'd signed and Rita signed.

In came the psychologists and the speech-language pathologists and the occupational therapists. They all saw Karen, most many times. They watched her in the classroom. They watched her on the playground. They made us fill out form after form, checklists of what we observed about our daughter. Yes, she did do some of the things on those forms, but she didn't do some of the others at all.

The day of the meeting Rita was a nervous wreck. Tad wasn't nervous, just ticked. He had to miss a big meeting, one where his potential commission would provide the down payment on their house. But this was his daughter and Rita insisted that it was important. He went. He didn't have to like it, but he went, and sat tilting back in his chair, his arms across his chest.

The bombshell fell. These twerps thought his kid, his beautiful, perfect little girl had autism. Autism! He pictured some guy huddled on the floor in the corner, rocking back and forth, making weird noises, lost in his own world. That was so, so far from his Karen. Had these people lost their minds?

He tuned back in. Oh, a form of autism. Well, big whoop. Autism was autism and that certainly was not Karen. He protested, "She's smart."

Heads nodded all around him. The psychologist agreed that yes, Karen was a very bright little girl. Her ability was at the ninety-fifth percentile, meaning that she scored lower than only about five percent of kids her age on the Weschler Intelligence Test for Children. See? Of course he'd known all along she was exceptionally intelligent.

But this group of so-called professionals got talking on and on about autism spectrum disorders, in particular something called Asperger's Syndrome. All Tad really got out of it was that Asperger's was something at the high functioning end of some spectrum. But now Rita was nodding.

They were talking about social impairments. Of course she was having some social problems; she was so far above the kids in her room that they couldn't relate to her, he told them. These people proceeded to give him example after example of Karen's defects in the social department. He could tell these people a thing or two about social skills. How dare they invite he and Rita into the school only to spend an hour running down their little girl? He got up to leave. "Coming, Rita?" he asked.

"No, not just yet. I think I'll stay and try to learn a bit more."

He'd stared at her, feeling her betrayal in his heart. If her parents wouldn't stand up for Karen, then who would? At least Karen still had her father in her court. And she always would.

Just then the phone rang, breaking his reverie.

He put his cell phone to his ear. "Hello."

"Dad?"

Once on the street, Jeff asked again, "Now what?"

Lori appreciated that unlike Jack, Jeff didn't take charge, demanding or controlling her. That did not seem to be Jeff's way. He listened, asked pertinent questions and offered opinions when asked. Then, it was back in Lori's court.

When she didn't respond, Jeff asked, "Do you think he's still in your apartment?"

Lori sighed. "Likely. He didn't leave before when I told him to. He says he needs a place to hide out."

"Do you want to go home?"

"I can't stand the thought of being in the same space as him. And, he's trashed my place. I love my home; it's my sanctuary. I don't have enough money to stay at a hotel more than a night or two; I gave Jack money and now my savings account is pretty low."

Behind them, the last lights in the bakery went out. They heard a car start up in the back alley - Ellie driving home.

"Thanks for listening, Jeff. I shouldn't take up any more of your time. You probably want to get home, too. I'll figure something out."

"I am heading home. Why don't you come with me? It's not that far to walk and you shouldn't be out here alone at night. You can figure things out from my place."

He crooked his elbow and held out his arm, his head tilted to one side. "Coming?"

Lori took his arm. She hated being so indecisive but going with Jeff was at least taking action. Besides, he was pleasant company.

Until she figured out what to do, Jeff's place seemed as good as any to wait it out.

The night was calm but chilly as they walked. Lori shivered, partly from the dampness, partly from worry.

"Cold?" Jeff asked. He passed Lori's right hand across the back of his waist, grasped it with his right and placed both their hands in the broad pocket of his jacket. The he slung his left arm over her shoulder, drawing her closer. "Better?"

Yes, this did feel better. The comfort of another person and this arm around her felt so different that when Jack did it last night. She wanted to cuddle into Jeff, unlike the revulsion she'd felt at Jack's closeness.

The lights were on in the living areas of his home but Jeff led them around to the side of the house, using his key to unlock the door, then they headed to basement. Jeff was nimble on the stairs, but Lori groped for handrails in the darkness. She called, "Jeff?"

"Sorry. I forgot it would be hard for you. I never turn on the light - it's fluorescent and flickers. I hate it." But he turned it on anyway for Lori.

A light was not needed in the basement. The glow from computer screens illuminated the crowded space. Many computer screens, monitor after monitor.

"Wow," Lori said. "What is this?"

"My home. I live here and I work here."

"I thought you worked at the bakery?"

"I do. But I also have coding, beta and regression testing contracts. And I like to play games." He grinned. "Before I started at the bakery, this is where I spent all my time."

Lori glanced around. The place resembled a computer lab, wires and cables snaking throughout the floor, chairs on casters ready to scoot between monitors.

Jeff sat at one of the screens and immediately became engrossed in the swirling data. Left to her own Lori wandered. Although she could use a computer and through herself fairly proficient, what she saw on the screens was incomprehensible to her.

Several times she turned to say something to Jeff, but he seemed lost in his data. She draped her coat over a chair and looked for a place to sit, out of the way of Jeff's rolling chair. Near one wall was a large, upholstered lounge chair, the kind with wide arms, a high back and enough length to stretch out her legs. As she pulled up her feet and sank into the space, it molded her body. She was not the first person to relax here. Her arms dangled over the sides of the chair, her fingers brushing a lever. She leaned over to take a look and gave the lever a pull. The back of the chair reclined slightly. Ah. She put her head back. She'd rest here a bit while she figured out what to do.

The sun attempted to make its way through the grimy windows. Lori turned over, stretching her arms. She opened her eyes, confused as to where she was. Her head swiveled to the tap, tap, tap sound - Jeff working on a keyboard.

It was morning. Her chair was fully reclined; there was a pillow beneath her head and a quilt over top of her. She wiggled her feet, noting that her shoes were off. Had Jeff tucked her in? She had certainly slept well, but what about Jeff. He was in the same position she'd seen him last night, staring at screens, clicking on his keys.

Lori got up, stretching. As she began walking around, he seemed to return to their world, noticing her. "Sleep well?" he asked. "Bathroom's through there," he pointed, "towels under the sink."

Lori headed off, wishing she had a change of clothing with her. Draped over the side of the tub was a folded pair of sweats and a t-shirt. They actually looked like women's and she wondered if this was a pair Mel had left here. She picked up the bundle and buried underneath was a pair of socks plus underwear, still in its packaging. Really? Would Jeff have thought of this?

She popped back into the main room, the clothes in her hand. "Jeff?" she asked.

He swiveled to face her. "Ah, I see you found the stuff. I got it from Mel's drawers upstairs. She won't mind if you use it. Mel says the rule is new shirt, socks and underwear every morning."

Lori blushed, but Jeff didn't notice. He'd turned back to the widescreen LCD screens. Lori hesitated, then she had to know. "Jeff, does your mother come down here?"

"Ha. Never. She's obsessively tidy and can't stand the way my place looks. And I'm obsessive about having my things just the way I like them. No, she never comes downstairs; we're both happier that way. Dad has bad knees and doesn't do stairs."

So, it must have been Jeff who took off her shoes and covered her up as she slept.

"Pumpkin!" Tad spoke into his cell phone.
"Dad, don't call me that. You know I hate orange."
"Sorry, Marigold."

"Daaaad," Karen groaned. "It's not nice to tease."

"All right, honey. I miss you."

"If you miss me, why are you there and not home?"

"We went over that. I have to work - a lot. There's not enough time to drive home."

"Not ever?"

Tad hemmed. "At least not for a while, Karen."

"I'm used to you being here. It's not the same. I want my daddy back."

"I am your daddy, Pumpkin. Always, no matter where I am. I love you."

"Your words don't match what you're doing."

Tad heard a clunk of the cordless phone hitting the table then a stomp down the hardwood hallway. He could picture his daughter stalking off in a snit.

The phone was picked up. "Tad?" Rita said. "I'm sorry about that. I didn't know what she was going to say. She just said that she wanted to phone you. I wouldn't have let her attack you when you're tired and working so hard. She doesn't understand." She almost added, "Neither do I," but kept that to herself.

Tad sighed. He could tell that Rita was trying. He knew she wasn't happy about his need to be away. He wondered if she was in denial about his reasons. "It's okay, Rita. This is hard for Karen, I know."

"It's hard for all of us." The words were neutral, without accusation.

For that, Tad was grateful. He didn't feel up to a battle with his wife tonight. His wife. Was she actually that or was she on her way to becoming his ex-wife? He knew that that was not what she wanted. He was the one pulling away. But not from Karen, never from his little girl.

"I wanted to talk with you anyway. I was going to wait until you got home, but you've not been back for a while." Rita's voice was carefully neutral. "You know how Karen's passion is cooking shows? Well, recently she's had this thing about chateaubriand. Her birthday's next month."

Come on, come on, thought Tad. Get on with it. Did she think he'd forgotten when his only child's birthday was? Or was she going to suggest some gift far out of their means?

"I thought that maybe the three of us could go out to a nice restaurant that serves chateaubriand."

Was this truly to do something for Karen, or was this Rita's way of trying to draw him back in? Chateaubriand. How much would that set him back? To put her off, he said, "I'll look into it when I have a minute. I'm not sure it's within our budget."

"I thought that I could look into who might have it and the cost. I have more time on my hands than you and I don't want to put even more on your plate."

"It can't hurt to find out prices, but no guarantees."

"Now that we're on the phone, there are a couple things I wanted to talk to you about. There's a counselor at Karen's school who knows something about Asperger's Syndrome and he works with parents. I've made appointments for half a dozen sessions with him. I thought it couldn't hurt and maybe we'll get some ideas to help Karen."

Tad thought about this. "Probably can't hurt. You can always cancel if you think the guy's a quack or talking through his hat. After all, we know our daughter best." There was a pause. "Although I don't get to spend as much time with her as I'd like these days."

"That's the other thing I wanted to talk about - just how much you're working."

Tad rolled his eyes and slouched deeper into the ratty couch." Rita, we've been over this. That's the job now. I have to work more to bring in the same amount of money. Or less. The market is getting harder each month. We'll likely need to cut back on expenses."

"I understand. I know we agreed that I'd stay home with Karen while she needed me. But she's older now and doing better. I don't think I need to be home all the time. And, I get lonely. I have too much time on my hands and thought I'd like to get a job." When this was met with silence, she hurried to add, "At least a part-time job."

"Where did this idea come from?"

"I've been thinking about it for a while. You're working so hard and I don't have enough to do. I could help out more, taking some of the pressure off you."

"Some extra money might be good. But that doesn't change things between you and I," Tad said.

Rita's small voice sounded like Karen's "I know." Rita refrained from admonishments or pleas. She was past that.

Neither spoke.

CHAPTER 10

As she dropped Kyle off for Little Chefs, Mel heard her name called.

Rita hurried along the hallway after Mel. "Hi again. Interested in going back to that coffee shop while we wait?"

Mel commented on Karen's glasses. Not only were they straight, but they were new and stylish. "Not a piece of tape anywhere on them," Rita confirmed. "And, we hadn't realized it, but Karen kept fiddling with those glasses because she couldn't see properly. She needed a prescription change. As much as I don't want my daughter ridiculed by other kids, if I hadn't overheard that incident a last week's Little Chef, we would never have known to get her new glasses."

"Karen seemed to have survived it just fine."

"She mentioned something else. The kids have been bugging her about her clothes. They mock her Dora shirts. She loves Dora. Even her lunch box has Dora on it. Why can't they just leave her alone? She likes what she likes."

Mel winced. "I know more about Dora than I ever cared to." The women shared a grin. "Kyle loves Dora as well. I'm sure he has every Dora movie memorized word for word. But, he's starting to grow out of this Dora phase and he's watching other things now as well. Did that happen to Karen?"

"Sort of, but she still likes Dora. For years now her favorite shirts all have the Dora pictures. The other day though, when she was eating breakfast, she got quiet then went upstairs to change. She came back down wearing a plain sweat shirt - no Dora anything on her that day."

"Wonderful! That's great news."

Rita tilted her head to one side, lowered one eyebrow and raised her cheek. "What?"

"You should be excited. That is real progress. She noticed what she wore and what her classmates said penetrated."

"No, that's not right. Why should my little girl have to bow to peer pressure? She should be able to wear whatever she wants."

"You said something important there - little girl. Dora is a big deal to little kids, but generally, as kids grow older, their tastes change." Mel dipped her spoon into the whipped cream topping her coffee. "What do you think interests other twelve year old girls?"

"The latest pop star sensation, I'd expect. But Karen's not like them. She's her own person."

"I applaud that. Being an individual is great, but there's a cost. Her classmates are laughing at her because they think Karen's interested in something babyish. This is a rough age. Kids are trying to separate from childhood and enter the teen years. On one side they see the pleasurable things they cherished when they were little. Then they see the enticing opportunities awaiting them as teenagers. They're torn - interested yet a bit scared of growing up. They want to be seen as older and to identify with teenagers more than with their younger counterparts. Karen hanging on to childish things like Dora is uncomfortably close to what some of those kids secretly still like. Karen's a reminder of what they used to be and are trying so hard to leave behind. I bet that two thirds of the grade six students loved Dora when they were four and five. But as they matured, they moved on to other things. But not Karen."

"So she's supposed to bow to whatever whim moves the other kids? What's wrong in liking what she likes? It doesn't harm anyone else."

"True, but it might be harming Karen. Socially, at least. It's fine to have an interest in whatever. Grown men build model airplanes and trains and meet in clubs to talk about it. But Karen's in a tricky position. She struggles socially anyway. She does not pick up on the social cues that other children absorb by osmosis."

"We've certainly noticed that. For a smart kid....".

"Remember when Steve made that comment about Karen's glasses? I don't think she got it until we showed her in a mirror how she looked."

"At the time I thought you were being cruel and mocking my daughter, but then I understood what you were trying to do. You helped her."

"I hope so. You're in the best position to help her, though. By dressing in a certain way, Karen is making herself a target for teasing."

"Isn't that like blaming the victim?"

Mel sighed. "Sort of. But that's reality. Chickens in a henhouse will pick on the one bird that looks different. Sadly, children can be similar. Karen's the only girl in grade six still wearing the kind of clothes you'd find in a kindergarten room."

"But she loves Dora. Those are the clothes she wants to wear. It's getting harder and harder though to find them for her. She's grown and they don't make a lot of Dora clothes in her size."

Mel gave her a pointed look. "There's a reason for that."

"I hadn't thought of it like that. I've also had to tell Karen to pull her pants up. She's grown and they slide down her bottom a bit. When she bends over her dad says she looks like a plumber."

"How do you know think the other kids will react if that happens at school?"

Rita grimaced. "It wouldn't be pretty."

"Karen may not even be aware of such possibilities or how she would look to the other kids. She needs someone to guide her and help her avoid some of these embarrassments."

"The way you did with her glasses."

"Similar, but you know her best and how to approach things."

"Tad's business has been hit hard by the downturn. We're not flush and buying all new outfits for Karen is not really in the budget."

"Goodness, no. That would not be reasonable, nor would it give Karen a good sense of money. She doesn't need everything new. Don't you ever shop at second hand stores?"

Rita pulled back and her eyebrows rose. "Never. Never thought of it."

"You'll be surprised what you find there and most of the sales go toward a good cause. You can donate your old clothes there at the same time."

"She doesn't need everything new. Some of her clothes are okay if they were just paired with other things. She's always collecting things so she could use her Dora lunch box to hold collections and I could get her plain one for school. But how will I explain this to Karen?"

"Tell her the truth, of course."

"What, that kids laugh at her."

Mel gave Rita's hand a squeeze. "I think she knows that already. What she doesn't know is why that happens. Telling her that it's her little girl clothes might help. Ask her to look at what the other girls in her room wear then report back to you about it. See which outfits appeal to her, then you'll have a basis to look for when you go shopping."

"I'll see what they have at Macy's."

"Why Macy's?"

"That's the only place we go. Ever since Karen was little, it was the only safe place to shop with her. It's quieter and the lighting doesn't seem to bother her. It was iffy anyplace else so we just stopped going."

"What if Macy's doesn't have what she wants?"

"Oh, they always do. I go earlier by myself to make sure. We don't go, otherwise."

"Hmmm." Mel didn't look pleased as they headed back to the school to pick up their kids.

There was a knock on Rob's open office door. "You must be Karen's mother. Come on in," he said, moving from behind his desk to shake hands with Rita.

"Thanks for seeing me. Mel suggested that you might have some ideas for helping my daughter."

"Sure. Or at least we'll see if we can come up with some together. I'm Rob Sells. I teach grade one here and I'm also the part-time guidance counselor. Have a seat." He gestured to the arm chairs or couch, waiting for Rita to choose.

Rita arranged her coat on the couch beside her fidgeted with her purse, then ran her scarf between her fingers several times before starting. "Karen's our only child and she means the world to us. We know she's different but she's special and very smart. We've done everything in our power to protect her."

When she paused, staring at the silk scarf, Rob guessed, "But it's not enough, right?"

A tear escaped and Rita wiped it away, hoping Rob had not noticed. "We have tried so hard, but Karen's not happy. She wants to be like other kids and wants to fit in, but she just doesn't."

"I hear she's in Little Chefs."

"Yes. That's the first group activity she's tried that's worked out. At least, so far it's worked out. They haven't asked her to leave, anyway."

"And they won't. I hear she's doing well and is an asset to the group."

Rita's radiant smile lit her face. She didn't often hear good things about her child. "Through Little Chefs I met Mel and she's been helpful. She's suggested some things and thought I should talk to you as well. Karen has Asperger's Syndrome." The last words came out in a rush. When Rob just nodded, she added, But she's smart, really smart."

"Is that why you're here?"

Rita was taken aback. "No, but I just wanted you to know."

"Anyone with a diagnosis of Asperger's has to have cognitive ability in the average or above average range. I think maybe the reason you're here is that just being smart isn't good enough."

Rita nodded, feeling almost guilty about the admission. But, she needed help and would do anything for Karen.

"Let's look back at some of what you said earlier. You mentioned how you and your husband have done your best to protect Karen."

Again, Rita nodded.

"Protecting can seem like the kind thing to do at the time, can't it? But there will come a time when you're not there to protect her. The key is to have made sure the child learned the skills she'll need to manage herself."

"We thought she would. We thought she just needed a bit more time to grow up in some areas and protecting her would give her that time. But we can't be with her all day at school to protect her from classmates. She gets so hurt by them and she doesn't know what she's done to make them pick on her. She ends up thinking she's a lousy person when she isn't. Really, she's a lovely child."

"Yes, she is. The problem is that she doesn't pick up on the social cues. That's common with kids on the autism spectrum disorder."

"So this is simply the way it is for her." Rita's shoulders drooped and she stared at the carpeting.

"Not at all. As you said, she's smart. She can learn. We can teach her some of the things that other kids picked up on her own."

"Where will she go to learn these things?"

"Anywhere. Your home, here at school, at the grocery store."

"Who will we get to teach her?"

"You will likely be her main teacher, plus her father. Then we'll help at school and she'll learn from the kids as well."

"It hasn't worked so far?"

"What if we turned our focus from protecting her from the world to learning how to deal with it?"

"How do we start," Rita wanted to know.

"Tomorrow's Saturday. What are your plans?"

Rita explained Mel's suggestion about changing Karen's wardrobe, emphasizing less Dora and more age appropriate clothing.

Rob asked, "Does Karen know why you're going shopping?"

Rita uncrossed and crossed them again the other way her legs, not meeting Rob's gaze. "Not really. She knows we're going shopping but probably assumes we'll look for more Dora clothes. I told her that hers are getting too small on her."

"Did you tell her or show her? There's a difference, you know."

"I told her. I know that Mel took Karen to the bathroom mirror and showed her why the kids laughed at her glasses. I wanted to snatch my daughter away from Mel before those words hurt her even more. But Karen wasn't insulted. She looked at herself and she got it."

"Right. Kids with autism spectrum disorders generally take in information that they see far easier than what they hear."

"Karen doesn't have autism. She has Asperger's," Rita protested.

"Asperger's is on the autism spectrum. The main difference between a child with Asperger's and a child with high functioning autism may be the age at which they acquired spoken language. By the time the kids are Karen's age, the differences may be indiscernible, depending on how severely the kid is affected by the autistic features."

"Asperger's sounds so much better. I don't mean to be a snob, but I don't want Karen lumped in with the common kid who has an autism diagnosis."

"The spectrum part of the label means two things - the severity of how the autism characteristics affect the individual and the wide range of cognitive ability of people on the spectrum. A child with a diagnosis of autism may have a profound intellectual disability or may have an IQ considerably above average."

"But the outcomes...."

"Because kids with Asperger's have intelligence in the normal range or above, in theory, they should have positive outcomes as adults. But in reality, only about one in ten young people with Asperger's lives independently."

Rita's eyes widened and her lips parted. "That's not going to be my Karen."

"Nope. None of us want that for her. We want all of her options open. We want her to be a strong, independent young woman, following her dreams."

"All those other young people, those stats. Did they not have parents who cared about them?"

"Many did and do. No, that's not the reason why they're unable to be independent as young adults."

Worried, Rita asked, "Why then? It must have been their schools."

"Nope. Many of them would have had concerned teachers, just like they had concerned parents. The research is still new that there aren't clear indicators. But one thing has become clear - many of these kids have been over-helped."

"Over-helped? How can you help someone too much?"

"By paving the way for them. By solving problems for them, by jumping in to prevent any frustrations, decisions or consequences. Depriving them of the opportunity to make a mistake and make choices and learn to trust their own judgment. To fail and go at it again. You know, all those things that other kids go through."

"But these kids are different. Things are harder for them. Just look at Karen. She's so smart but she has trouble fitting in. She has no friends. Some days you can read the stress in her body. Kids like Karen need to be protected."

"I've seen smart kids like Karen who do very well academically all through school. They are helped and shielded by their teachers and parents. Then grade twelve is over and all those school supports disappear. It's time to either get a job or delve into post-secondary education. IQ-wise, they're up for either, or they should be."

"And why wouldn't they?" Rita asked.

"Because being smart isn't good enough. You need adaptive skills to enable you to use your smarts. Many Asperger's kids try college but drop out."

"Why? They have the brains to do it."

"Yes, but again, being smart isn't enough. Our liberal arts colleges don't demand classes in just one area, that of the student's interest. For example, take computers. A kid may be totally focused on computers and be highly skilled. But to get a degree, he or she also needs to take classes in Mathematics, and Science and English. Often these Aspie kids aren't in the habit of having to do things they don't want to do."

"Already Karen doesn't like to do assignments in school that don't interest her. We think she's bored with some of them because she's so much smarter than her classmates."

Rob gave her a look.

"I know, I know," Rita conceded. "Some of the other kids must be bright, too."

"Definitely. Sometimes a kid has not had enough life experience or experience in that subject to understand why she's asked to do certain assignments. Maybe it's a required part of the curriculum that just doesn't interest her. It still has to be done."

"Karen hates that, especially when it's not her idea. You should see when we play board games at home. She has to win or life is just too unpleasant for all of us. When she doesn't like the game's rules, she makes up her own and we play by them."

"Hmmm. Does that help her?"

"Well, she wins and she's happy."

"As far as I can see, it's just plain harder to raise a child who has an ASD. It's more work. Everything becomes a teaching situation. So when you and your husband play board games like that with Karen, what is she learning?"

"To have fun with her family."

"True, but on whose terms?"

"Oh, definitely on Karen's terms," admitted Rita.

"What if we pull that same board game out at school and Karen plays with her classmates. How do you think they'll react to having to play by Karen's rules? And, will they let her win?"

"Doubtful. They're usually mean to her." She paused a minute. "I get what you're saying. We thought we were building up her self-image by letting her win, building her confidence and having fun as a family."

"I understand why you did it. Wouldn't it be easier for Karen to learn how to lose in the security of her family? No one goes through life without losing sometimes. As hard as it may be to deal with when you're twelve, imagine how it feels to first experience failure when you're twenty?"

Rita thought about what their next game of monopoly would look like if Karen wasn't given the properties she wanted. She shook her head. 'Twouldn't be pretty.

"How did your shopping trip with Karen go last weekend?" Rob asked Rita.

"It was different than anything I've done with her in a long time. Usually I go to the store ahead of time to make sure that they have what Karen wants. That way we won't have any upsets."

"And?"

"I know we talked about not sheltering her, helping her build the skills she'll need to manage and how things in life don't always work the way we'd like. Well, that certainly happened." Rita sighed before continuing. " I tried your suggestion and we just went shopping. I was a nervous wreck."

"Was Karen a nervous wreck?"

"No, she had no idea this was any different from other times we went shopping at Macy's. She never knew that I'd always scouted things out ahead of time."

Rob grinned and nodded his encouragement.

Rita said, "Just as I feared, Macy's did not have any Dora shirts in Karen's size. You'll be pleased to know that I let her figure this out on her own. She found some Dora tops and I suggested she look at the size. She picked the ones she wanted then I insisted that she go into the change room to try them on. I didn't go in with her the way I usually would. Actually, Karen's hardly ever been in a change room. Usually I'd know which things would probably fit and just buy them. At home Karen would try them in her room then I'd return the items if they didn't feel comfortable to her."

"And this time?" Rob asked.

"I was outside the change rooms talking with a saleslady. We heard these grunting, then some wails and a shriek or two. Karen couldn't pull the shirts over her head, they were that small for her. I pretended that I didn't hear the noises even though the saleslady kept glancing over my shoulder. Then, I don't think the woman could stand it because she went to Karen's door and asked if she needed any help. I tried to stay out of it. You should have seen my daughter. She and the saleswoman worked it out. When none of the Dora shirts would fit, I asked the woman what she'd recommend for Karen. Then I backed out and let the two of them have at it. We ended up with some nice things, clothes I'm pretty sure other girls her age would wear."

Rob started to speak, but Rita held up her hand.

"That's not all," she said. "The saleslady talked about these certain jeans they were all out of, but she'd seen some in another store in the mall. Karen listened to her, and we actually shopped in a couple other stores. The food court threw her for a bit because it was so noisy, but she managed. I think we broke the bank that day and spent far more than we should, but it was such a great day - our first mother/daughter shopping spree. Now I think I need to get a job to help pay off that credit card bill."

"What kind of a job, or were you just kidding?"

"Partly I was kidding, but seriously, I've been thinking about it a lot lately. Before we had Karen, we agreed that I would be a stay-at-home mom, raising our child. Then for years it was obvious that Karen needed more care and attention than other kids so we never questioned being a one-income family."

"And now?"

"Now, Karen's growing up. And, money is tight for us. This economic downturn really hit hard in Tad's line of work. He needs to put in far more hours to make the sales he used to. Often, despite the extra work, he's bringing in less in commissions than before. He's working so much we hardly ever see him anymore. It's hard on Karen and it's hard on us as well."

"What kind of work are you thinking of?"

"I've worked a bit in retail sales years ago and it was so so. I started a course in library science at one time but dropped out when I became pregnant with Karen."

"I took my grade one class to the public library last week. I noticed that they had a help wanted sign on their door."

"You mean the library over on Third and Maple?"

Rob nodded.

"That's walking distance from our house. Karen could even meet me there after school and stay until I finished work." She thought a minute then said, "I wonder what Tad would say about the idea."

"Karen gets so down on herself. We worry about her," Rita confessed at their next appointment.

"What indication does she give that tells you she's down on herself?" Rob asked.

"She's pretty obvious. She huffs and flounces around, pouts and says how stupid she is."

"When does she do this?"

"When something hasn't gone her way, when she tries something that doesn't come easily to her or when she doesn't live up to expectations."

"Whose expectations? Yours or hers?"

"Well, both. I don't know, they're one and the same, aren't they?"

"That depends. Let's talk a bit about her smartness."

Rita settled back, comfortable with this topic.

"In what ways is Karen smart?" Rob asked.

"It's her mind. She knows so much and when she finds a topic that interests her she researches it intently. And, she retains what she reads. She can tell you more about some subjects, like cooking, than the average adult will ever know."

"True. I've noticed that about her."

"And language. Her vocabulary has always been so advanced for her age."

"What is she not so good in?"

"Math. You know, for someone with a terrific memory like she has, she had a really hard time memorizing times tables. Something simple like that threw her. And time. She's just now getting good with digital time; for a while she'd read off the numbers but they didn't seem to have any meaning for her, other than a few set things like her bed time. But she still can't tell time on an analog clock." Rita thought some more. "If you're talking about school subjects, her worst is probably physical education. Sometimes she's a klutz and she doesn't get the rules of the games very easily. She's always throwing the ball the wrong way then the kids yell at her."

"Sounds like she's good at some things and not so good at others."

"She's good at the things that matter."

"Such as?"

"Well, her brain. She's smart. We've agreed on that."

"Yes. Unfortunately, being smart isn't good enough." Rob grinned. "I sound like a broken record about that, don't I?" He waited a couple seconds before continuing. "Let's go back to what you were saying about Karen getting down on herself when she doesn't do as well as she expected."

"A couple times in class she has not scored the highest mark. She checks with the other to be sure she's the best, but there are a few kids who have beaten her on occasion. She hates that. The last time she cried in class and everyone made fun of her."

"Sometimes kids tie up their self-worth with their marks. You're already seeing where that can lead. Some kids feel that they're only valued when they're on top and being second best or even lower means they're a failure as a person."

Rita blanched. "We've been trying to help Karen feel good about herself by praising her marks."

"I wonder if you could show her that you're proud of her when she gets good grades, but you're proud of other aspects of her personality as well."

"We are. Of course we love everything about our daughter."

"Does she know that? Sometimes kids misconstrue what we convey and end up feeling their only worthy when they reach some accomplishment or expectation."

"Of course she knows that we love her, no matter what."

"Good, because I've seen kids pick up messages that their well-meaning parents did not intend to give. Some kids think that they're valued for what they can do, rather than for who they are. If that doesn't fit Karen, that's great." Rob let the silence hang.

"We'll check with Karen and make sure she knows she doesn't have to be perfect."

"Before, when we talked about where you see your daughter in five or ten years, you definitely thought she was college bound. Once there, she'll be up against kids who are as bright as she is, maybe brighter. She won't necessarily be at the top in all of her classes, something that comes as a rude shock to some students. On average, kids see their marks fall by maybe ten percent in college, compared to what they were used to in high school. That's hard on the ego if the kid has not had some experience with failure or not doing as well as hoped and learning how to cope with that kind of disappointment. You have six years to help prepare her."

"Tad and I have been reading up on resiliency since we talked about it a few weeks ago. This is all part of building a resilient kid. We want her to be able to rise to challenges and to handle the things life throws at people."

"Independently?"

"Definitely. Tad reminded us that we might not be around to shelter her all the time. Thinking back to how we both were in our late teens, she might not want our help. And, if she ends up living with us when she's finished high school, we want it to be because she wants to, not because she's unable to manage living on her own."

CHAPTER 11

Rob began their fifth session. "It sounds like there have been lots of changes in your household. How is Karen reacting to her new responsibilities?"

Rita's smile was rueful. "About as well as you'd expect any adolescent to appreciate being made to do chores. But, we're doing it and sticking to it."

"Which ones is she doing now?"

"The first couple times she thought doing her own laundry was fun. As a little kid she liked sorting and lining up her toys. She handled her clothes in the same way, but over-sorted, not just the whites from the colored clothes, but she put all the clothes of each color together to wash each separately. Then she got stuck on whether her turquoise shirt should actually be in with her green socks or her blue pants. If I'd let her, she would have had a dozen loads of laundry, each with just a few items. She was not a happy camper when I told her the rule was two loads and not more. Everything had to fit into one of two categories."

Rob grinned back at her. "Did it get easier?"

"Marginally. She still tries to argue with me about categories of colors, but we're holding fast to two loads."

Rob was about to speak, but Rita rushed on. "Oh, and the other thing she doesn't like is the dryer buzzer. The rule is that she has to remove her clothes from the dryer when the buzzer goes and hang them up so they don't get wrinkled. She gets engrossed in things and doesn't want to leave when she hears the buzzer."

"What do you do?"

"Tell her, 'The rule is....' and it works. I pretend I can't hear her grumbling," said Rita. "And I told you how she liked to line up her toys when she was younger. Well, she still likes things orderly and her closet organizer makes that easier. She used to like the way I hung up her shirts for her, all facing the same way, all centered on their hangers. The first time she did it herself, she was in a hurry to get back to a cooking show on television, so she just threw things on the hangers. When she returned to her room later, you'd have thought she was injured. She yelled and fussed and wailed about how her closet looked. She wanted me to fix it."

"Did you?"

"No way. Once I would have - anything to prevent her from being so distressed. But I just reminded her that it was her closet and her clothes. She could leave them the way they were or straighten them if she wished. Then I walked out. I had to lock myself in the bathroom and turn on the shower so I wouldn't hear her and be tempted to go do the rescuing thing."

"Excellent. And is she proud of herself now?"

"Proud? I'm not sure. But she does see herself as more grown up doing her own laundry. And, I think she might be a little less obsessive about the appearance of her closet. Mind you, I like her being neat, but it was getting to be a bit hard to take."

"Anything else you're working on?" Rob asked.

"Yes. I had a call from Mrs. Stewart complaining that Karen was not completing her work. Some of her work, that is. She only wanted to do some assignments. She refused to participate in their novel study, saying it was a stupid book and didn't make any sense. She only wanted to read nonfiction."

"That's not uncommon with kids on the autism spectrum. Nonfiction deals in straight facts. Fiction involves understanding character motivations, which means you have to be able to put yourself in their shoes - a tough task for most kids on the spectrum."

"I know. We had this problem last year. It upset Karen so much that I talked to the teacher and got her excused from anything to do with novels. She read extra nonfiction books instead and wrote reports on them - good reports."

"Did you ask Mrs. Stewart to excuse Karen?"

"Nope. We're not sheltering her. Tad said he didn't get any say in what he was required to read in college, so we'd better start preparing Karen now."

"Even if it's hard for her, learning about other people's thoughts through reading fiction is useful. She'll learn a lot about interpreting other's thoughts and feelings and gain skills in analyzing why people might behave the way they do."

"My daughter would much rather deal with black and white facts."

"It's those fuzzy grey areas where she needs practice, doesn't she?"

"I don't know how to teach those things."

"You've started with things like her closet. She's learning to tolerate things that are not quite perfect. You didn't hold her hand through all those laundry sorting decisions. Karen's learning to handle ambiguity and to even handle the odd mistake as happened when her red socks found their way into her white load."

"I can laugh about it now, but I sure didn't at the time. None of us did. Telling her that everyone has made that mistake at some time didn't help her. She felt she should be perfect. You can bet she checks her white load carefully now."

Rob chuckled. "I slept in pink sheets my first year away from home."

"Back to Mrs. Stewart. We made a plan. I'd make it clear to Karen that her job as a student was to do the work the teacher assigned. Karen went on and on about how stupid the book was and how there were better books and she wasn't going to waste her time on any old novel someone just made up out of their head."

Rita continued, "So I told her that Mrs. Stewart was emailing me after school to let me know if Karen had completed that day's assignment. If she had, great. If she hadn't finished it during school time, then it was homework. The assignment must be completed and completed properly before any cooking shows could be watched. You know how Karen loves those shows and watches them every single day."

"How'd it turn out?"

"The first day she came home without having finished her work. She thought she was off the hook because she *forgot* her books at school. She tried to turn on the television. I stood in front of her with my coat on and hers in my hand. We were heading right back to school to get her things." Rita grinned at Rob. "As you can imagine, it was not a fun drive. But things got worse. Back in the house Karen was slamming around and howling about how unfair life was. After supper she pulled out her books grudgingly when she saw that I wasn't going to cave on this. Maybe my timing was bad, but I explained how she'd taken twenty minutes of my time when I had to drive her back to school. So now she owed me twenty minutes. I figured that's about how long it would take her to do the dishes, so I added that to what had to be done before she could watch television."

"Wow! You're tough. Way to go, mom." Rob gave her a high five.

"By the time Karen finished her homework and the dishes, it was almost bed time. She only had time for the last half of one cooking show. But I stuck to my guns. I reminded her that once she actually got down to her work, it only took her less than half an hour. She'd wasted most of the evening complaining.

"So, how have things been going the past few weeks," asked Rob. This was the last session Rita had booked with the school counselor.

"Good. Well, mostly good."

"With a pre-teen in the household, I think mostly good is as good as most people hope for."

"Nice to be considered normal, then. Yes, it's been generally good. I don't know why I didn't try some of this stuff before."

"Maybe Karen wasn't ready. Maybe you weren't ready before."

"Perhaps. I used to be afraid to rock the boat and would do anything in my power to keep Karen happy. Now, I'm not doing much of what I used to do and you know, Karen is not any less happy. Oh sure, we went through some pretty rough patches when I started to change and who is happy having to do stuff like laundry? But Karen adjusted more quickly than I would have thought; at least once she realized that I wasn't going to back down. As we were going through that, I tried to do what you suggested - take a step back, stop talking and just observe.

" And you know what?" Rita continued. "It wasn't pretty. Ever seen a twelve year old throw a two year old tantrum? Watching her in the throes of it, I could see her little two year old self ten years ago. Yikes, it scared me. Was this what my daughter had become? Was this what I had made her into?"

Luckily for Rob, he only had time to smile before Rita carried on.

"My having a job was particularly tough on Karen. I no longer had as much time to be at her beck and call. She didn't like it, but she could see the sense in my expecting her to pitch in with chores since I wasn't at home all day anyway. Oh, she whined lots and grumbled about my job and things changing, but she got over it. And, she likes the extra money we now have for things since she's developed a sudden interest in clothes and shopping."

"Are you okay with that? " Rob asked.

Rita smiled. "It's nice to be doing a typical mother-daughter thing. I see other moms and kids at the mall and we don't look too different. In fact, no one stares or pays us any attention. That's a switch since Karen now dresses like any other girl her age."

"So, it's all working out for you?"

"The biggest hurdle for Karen was having to share my time. It used to be that all my attention was focused on her. I'd sit at home alone all day, just waiting for her to get home from school. I'd hang on her every word. Really, I think I was starved for company, especially with Tad being away so much of the time."

"Sounds like your world was constricting."

"I didn't think about it at the time, but looking back, yes, it was. And somehow, I think I was using my daughter to fill a void."

Rita got up and walked to the window. Gazing out on the playground, she thought a minute before turning back around. "There's a big world out there. I had not realized how ours had narrowed - Karen's and mine, especially without Tad around. I clung to my daughter; there should never be a kid's role. It's different now. I'm different now. I like having a job. I meet interesting people; I'm doing something useful, something I'm good at. And, it feels nice to contribute to the family income. It's also healthy for Karen to see that much as I love her, I do have a life that does not always revolve around her. I think I'm a more interesting mother now, a less needy and more interesting person."

"It looks like Karen is blossoming under your guidance and the choices you've made."

"I have you to thank for encouraging me to make some of these choices and helping me find the courage. Both Karen and I are better for it."

"I need to work on Tad and me now. I don't know if things will work out for us, but I now know that we'll be all right either way."

"Watch me, dad." Karen did a cartwheel down the hall. Or what Tad guessed was supposed to be a cartwheel. She had it right with the arms - both hit the floor. But one leg followed the bent knee smacking the wall. The other leg hung horizontally for a second before responding to gravity with a thud.

"Been practicing, princess?"

"Daaaad. That was my first time. They might start a gymnastics club at school and I'm thinking about joining."

Tad looked toward the kitchen where his wife stood with her arms crossed, leaning against the counter. They shared a smile, both delighting in the progress Karen was making.

"Good to hear. There are a lot of things you'll be able to do with practice."

This was the first weekend in months that Tad had made the trek home. It was Karen's birthday and they had reservations at the bakery for dinner. Jeff had managed it and Ellie advertised a chateaubriand night. The price was a bit more than the family would usually pay for a dinner, but nothing like restaurants Rita had scoped out. Besides, money was not quite as tight these days since Rita had started her job at the library.

"What are you wearing to your birthday dinner?" Rita asked Karen.

"That dress the saleslady helped me pick out."

Tad raised his eyebrows and mouthed to Rita, "A dress?" He had never seen his little girl in a dress, at least not since she'd been old enough to dress herself.

Rita nodded and smiled. "I think you'll be pleasantly surprised when you see it. Your little girl is growing up."

"No more Dora clothes?" Tad asked.

"Dad, Dora is for kids. I'm almost a teenager, I mean I will be in eleven months, thirty days and...," she paused a second,"...six hours and thirty four minutes." Then she added, "I still like Dora, but I just do Dora things when I'm home here by myself."

The nearest they could park was a block and a half away from the bakery. Never had Rita seen so many cars along the street. Good thing they had tickets for the dinner tonight and didn't leave getting a table to chance.

The bakery had been transformed. Always comfortable, it now had a sophisticated air. The lighting was dimmer, the classical music quiet and soothing. The round, glass tables were each draped with starched, white tablecloths, each place setting graced with a cloth napkin design.

Mel, playing hostess, greeted them at the door. "Hello Rita and Karen. We're delighted to have you with us tonight. I understand that you're not just here for the food, but this is a special celebration."

"It's my birthday," burst Karen. "And, my dad's home for the weekend." She beamed at her parents.

Tad held out his hand. "You seem to know my family. I haven't had the pleasure yet."

There was an edge to Tad's voice, Karen thought. Well, what did he expect, that their lives wouldn't go on without him if he chose to absent himself? "Tad, this is Mel Wickens, one of the teachers at Karen's school and sister-in-law to the owner of this bakery. Mel, I'd like you to meet my husband, Tad."

Mel shook Tad's hand. "We've enjoyed getting to know your wife and daughter. They're delightful to have around, aren't they?"

Tad colored slightly. "That's what I always say."

Karen looked at him. "Always? I don't remember hearing you say that."

"It's just a figure of speech, Karen."

As his daughter was about to delve into this some more, Mel interrupted. Taking Karen by the shoulders, she turned her towards a cozy corner where a table for three was decorated with flowers. Attached to one chair was a set of helium balloons floating in the breeze from the ceiling fan. Each balloon carried a birthday wish. "Guess which table is reserved for you," Mel asked.

The meal was as scrumptious as Jeff predicted and the bakery was full. There was no shortage of conversation at Blackwell family's table. After all, Karen had a lot to catch her absentee father up on.

But, Tad noticed a difference. No longer did Karen spout on and on; she actually came up for a breath. And, surprise, surprise, she asked a question and waited for the answer. This was new, this having a real conversation with his daughter, rather than listening, or half-listening to her monologue. Rita was mostly silent, but watched their daughter with quiet pride.

Her eyes met Tad's. Silently they acknowledged the changes in their child and smiled. Tad reached out and squeezed his wife's hand as it lay beside her wine glass. Over Karen's bowed head, he mouthed, "You've done a great job with her." Karen turned her hand over and linked her fingers with Tad's.

Karen was not the only to have changed in the last months. Tad noticed a difference in Rita as well. Maybe it was having her job at the library or maybe it was getting out of the house more. There was a quiet confidence about her, a sense of herself that had seemed missing for a long time. Or, maybe it had always been there, but *he* had been missing for a long time. They parents held hands as they let Karen decide the desserts they'd all sample.

CHAPTER 12

Lori noticed that Jeff was pretty much in the same position he had been when she'd fallen asleep last night. "Did you go to bed?" she asked.

"For a couple hours." He waved in the direction of the rumpled day bed in the corner. I looked the same way it did when they had entered the room last night. "I have a contract due and needed to get some heavy coding done."

Lori's rumbling stomach was audible above the hum of all the electronics in the room.

"I guess that's our cue. Let's go upstairs and we'll feed you."

Lori had heard sounds and footsteps from above since she'd awoken. "Are your parents there?"

"Just my mom. Dad's left for work already."

"Won't your mother think it funny to see me. Won't she assume..."

"Assume?"

"That I slept over."

"You did sleep over."

"No, I mean that I slept slept." She was glad that her blush would be hidden in the dim light coming in through the small, grimy windows.

"Although I often don't, most people do sleep at night."

"I've never met your mother and I'm not sure this is the way I want to for the first time. I think I'd better just leave."

Jeff rose and grabbed his jacket from the back of his chair. "Then let's go get something to eat somewhere else."

They ended up walking back to the bakery since it was the closest place and, as Jeff pointed out, it had the best food.

Lori looked at her watch. "Hey, aren't you supposed to be at work there?" she asked.

"Usually, but not today. Ellie knew I have this contract to complete." He held the bakery door open for Lori. The sound of the milk steamer greeted them along with the yeasty smells of bread fresh from the oven.

"Jeff! What are you doing here?" Ellie had not expected him.

"I needed to feed Lori and she didn't want to meet my mom."

The halogen spotlights of the bakery didn't hide Lori's blush this time. Ellie looked from one to the other of them but didn't comment. She waved toward the back room at Jeff. "Be my guest."

Ellie brought coffee for herself and Lori to the table. Lori looked down into the cup and blew into the steam, giving her reddened face time to get back under control. She wasn't a child and didn't owe anyone an explanation for having spent the night at Jeff's. She didn't know why people jumping to conclusions about any relationship between her and Jeff should bother her. She looked up to find Ellie studying her.

"I'm surprised to see Jeff here. He told me he was taking the day off to work on some big coding contract he had to finish. You have some powers if you could drag him away from that."

Bad subject. Lori needed to distract her. "I thought you relied on Jeff's cooking here. How do you manage without him?"

Jeff arrived with his own coffee and two plates of fresh croissants and brie. "Not well would be the answer to that question."

Ellie laughed. "True, but we stumble along as long as we've planned ahead. Right?"

"Right. We've worked it out now, but Ellie sure can get mad."

Lori looked between the two with a question in her glance.

Ellie explained. "The first time Jeff didn't show up, I was furious. We'd just gotten rolling and customers were starting to count on his concoctions for lunch. It was getting later and later and still no Jeff to get the meat cooking for sandwiches. I called and left messages and texted him, but no response. Jeff doesn't answer the phone when he's coding; doesn't even hear it, I'd suspect. Lunch service was a disaster and I had to turn customers away. There were only a few left-overs from the day before and those went fast. Then I had nothing but some cheese to use for sandwiches."

"The next day when I came into work, you should have seen Ellie. Probably you heard her all the way to the school. I didn't get what the big deal was. She knew I had other work I had to do. Or, I thought she knew. Ellie informed me that she could not read my mind and had no idea I wouldn't be showing up for work."

Ellie rolled her eyes. "Jeff explained to me about the Theory of Mind problem in people with autism and Asperger's, how they tended to assume that whatever was in their mind was also known to other people. He knew he had to work on his contracts so he assumed that I would know about that too." She shook her head in frustration.

"We've worked it out," Jeff said. "Now when I know that I have a contract coming up and can't be at the bakery, I tell Ellie ahead of time plus I cook extra the days before so El will have food to serve her customers." He leaned closer to Lori and lowered his voice a notch. "Before I started working here, you know, Ellie was in trouble. She wasn't getting enough business and the bakery was struggling. But my food changed that and she relies on me to bring in the lunch and dinner crowds."

Lori shot a quick glance at Ellie to see how she reacted to Lori being privy to this information.

"It's true," Ellie agreed. Jeff's skills have turned this place around."

Jeff stirred raw cane sugar into his dark coffee. "What's your next plan?"

"Plan?" Lori pretended she didn't know what he was getting at.

"Your next way of avoiding going back to your apartment?"

Busted, Lori thought. If only she knew for sure that Jack had left. "I guess I could phone and see if he's still there." The phone rang and rang until her answering machine picked up. That must mean he wasn't there.

"Want me to go with you?" Jeff offered.

Feeling like she was going all girly-girly Lori first said no, she was fine, then, "Maybe, just in case." She hated herself for feeling scared to enter her own home. This was Jack, the boy she'd skinned knees with as a child, the young man who'd rescued her when she was a teenager. He might be rough around the edges, but he'd never hurt her. He would though, take her money and take over her life whenever he popped back in. She straightened. "No, I'm fine on my own. I can do it alone."

"How long are you going to let him do this to you?" Jeff asked.

Conversations might be more comfortable if Jeff spoke with more tact. Or any tact. But maybe it was not tact she needed right now, but a friend backing her up. "I want him out of my apartment. Then I want him out of my life."

"Do you need back-up? I can come with you and we can get Ben to come, too." While Lori thought about this he added, "Did you think about calling the police?"

"Oh, no, I couldn't do that. Jack says he's hiding out, but I'm not sure from whom. He says he wants nothing to do with the police."

Jeff gave her a pointed look. "And that tells you...?"

Lori rose and pushed in her chair. "I need to get this over with. I can't be afraid to go to my own home." She glanced down at what she was wearing. "And, I can't continue to wear Mel's clothes."

"Want me to walk you home?"

"Nope. I'm fine. I'm going to do this. Thanks for everything." Jeff stood as Lori turned and walked out the door.

Ellie came to stand beside Jeff, watching Lori's retreating back. "What was that all about?" she asked.

"Lori has a plan."

As she rounded to hall to her apartment door, the noise, audible from the elevator, reached hit-in-the-head-with-a-watermelon proportions. Apartment 7C's door opened. Lori could see but not hear the thump, thump of Mrs. Hust's walker. Nor could she hear the words from her elderly neighbor's mouth, but she got the gist. With a nod and a quick hug, she reassured Mrs. Hust that she'd take care of it.

Standing in front of her door, Lori squared her shoulders and raised her bowed head. She could do this. She would do this. She raised her hand to rap then thought, what am I doing? This is my place. She dug in her pocket for her key, twisted the lock and pushed. The door budged an inch, just enough to let out even more ferocious music, then caught on the chain. Lori pounded on the door. When that didn't help, she took in deep breaths, and yelled with all her lungs' capacity to be heard over the raucous sounds. Nothing.

She put her ear to the door, trying to distinguish sounds. What was that behind the music? There were thumps, and grunts and noises that sounded like furniture moving. Or falling. Was he destroying her place? She put her lips to the crack in the door and screamed, "Jack!"

The door pushed back in her face, scraping her nose, then it opened fully, pulling her weight with it. She stumbled into her apartment and would have fallen on her face had not a hairy hand grabbed her arm. A voice said, "Is this the little woman?"

Lori raised her eyes from the scuffed, thick-heeled leather boots. The guy's belly protruded almost a foot over the massive belt buckle. Ragged strands of greasy hair clung to his forehead and cheeks, escaping from the azure scarf covering his head. He had her arm in a painful grip, pulling her close enough that she smelled the sour breath coming from between the yellowest teeth she'd ever seen. He gave Lori's arm an ungentle shake.

Her eyes took in her home, her cozy oasis. As angry as she'd been about the plant Jack had overturned, that was nothing compared to the current destruction. The vases she's scooped up from garage sales were shattered, the plants they'd held in varying degrees of tatter. Dishes lay smashed on the kitchen floor, their contents splattered. She had not realized she owned that many plates. Jack must have dirtied every one.

Jack! It took a minute to recognize the crumpled heap in the corner, mostly covered by the crocheted comforter that usually warmed the back of the recliner. His head and one shoulder slumped against the wall, the rest of his shirtless body wedged in between the corner and the recliner. He shook his head, raised marginally up on one elbow then slid back down with a groan.

She knew she should rush to his side to check on his condition but something held Lori back. This was not her fault. Whatever destruction there was to her place and to his body was brought on by Jack, not her. Body. Her attention jerked back to the lug gripping her arm. Was her body in danger as well? She took in the third man in the room, one whose hairy chest peeked through the leather vest held together by a cord wound through straining button holes. He too had on the same type of head scarf. He lounged against the wall beside the kitchen, one knee cocked and the toe of his boot resting on the floor while he picked under his fingernails with a knife. Was that the butcher knife from the block she kept on the counter? She could never use that again.

She was sick of this, oh so sick of Jack dropping into her life, taking her money and wreaking havoc. This was it - the last time. She drew herself up as tall as her five foot three frame would allow, turned to Jack, and extended her free hand toward the open door to the hall. "Out!" she shouted. "Get out right now. Out! And, don't ever come near me again." She jerked her arm away from the ape holding on to her. Maybe he'd expected her to weep or plead in his arms, but he let her go.

He laughed at Jack and shoved his fingertips into the back pockets of his sagging jeans. "Your little woman doesn't seem happy to see you."

She turned on him. "Who the hell are you and why are you in my apartment?" Then, before he could speak, she said, "Never mind. Just get out. Get out now." She gestured towards Jack. "And take that, that thing with you."

"Well, well. I guess you weren't stringing us along, were you Jack. She doesn't act like a devoted main mama." He looked over at his buddy. "Since she's not attached to anyone, do you think we should have some fun?" His friend pushed his bulk off the wall and approached.

Lori stomped over to her iPod docking station and turned down the racket. Wait. That wasn't her music. She tore the iPod off her station, clutching it in her hand. In the sudden silence, her words were fierce as she strode to the body of her old childhood friend. She threw the iPod at him with as much force as her biceps would give. It bounced off his cheek, opening up yet another rivulet of blood. This time her voice was less strident but shaking with conviction. "You get up and get out of here right now and never come back. How dare you do this to my place? Any debt I ever had to you is over, paid in full. Now, leave." She turned to the other men. "Get out of my apartment now!" Her voice rose on the last word.

She turned her back on the men as they each grabbed one of Jack's forearms and dragged him across the floor towards the door. As he slid past her, Jack's eyes fluttered then rested on Lori. "Sorry," his hoarse voice said.

"So, sorry."

Lori extended her arm towards the door. "Never again. We're done."

Jack nodded his head then his eyes drifted shut as the men hoisted him to his feet, slinging one of his arms around each of their shoulders.

As Lori watched their progress, she noticed movement in the open doorway. There stood Jeff, shoulder to shoulder with Ben. Behind them, Rob Sells' head peeked between their heads.

"I told you I didn't need any help." She glared at Jeff.

"No, I see that you didn't," replied Jeff, stepping back to let the men pass into the hallway.

"But at least we can clean up the mess," said Ben, trying to be diplomatic.

"Geez, Lori," said Rob. "At school you're pretty organized. I didn't realize you'd keep your place like this."

Lori's fists clenched and she gritted her teeth. She spun and stomped into the bathroom, locking the door behind her. Peeling off her clothes, she started the shower. The pounding of the water blocked out the sounds of the men hauling away the broken and tattered remnants of Lori's life in her secure haven. She leaned her head against the shower wall, letting the cleansing, warm water flow over her. I did it, she thought. I'm finally rid of Jack and his influence over me. So what if I lost my beautiful home - that was just stuff. I stood up to Jack. She remembered the mantra 'You don't have to be a victim'. She was strong. Only then did the tears come.

When she had wrung every possible drop of warm water out of the shower, Lori emerged, wrapped in her floor-length, white terry-cloth robe, her wet hair in a turban. Expecting to see the men still carting off debris, she was startled to see Mel, Ellie and Mel's mother.

"When Ben texted me about the condition of your place, Ellie and I came over. Once I saw that he wasn't exaggerating, I knew there was no one more efficient at cleaning than my mom," said Mel. "Lori, I'd like you to meet my mother, Doreen Nicols. Mom, this is Lori Nabaker. She and I work closely together at school. She's a friend of Jeff's, too."

The women shook hands, then Lori turned to Ellie. "How can you be here? What about the bakery?"

"Suze is there and I called in my parents. They can't build a decent cappuccino, but they can wait tables and do dishes. They love to be needed and dad will be in his glory bustling about, thinking he owns the place again. Besides, you needed help."

Jeff, Ben and Rob had carted off most of the broken items and swept the floor. Doreen waved Lori away. "Off with you to get some clothes on and we'll get started in here. Take your time, dear. With four of us, this won't be such a bad job. Mel, see what you can salvage of these gorgeous plants. If they're too broken, take cuttings and I'll root them at home. We'll get her going again with greenery. Ellie, go with Lori. She might be distraught over the state of her bedroom. Take this trash bag and gather up all the laundry that needs to be done. I'll tackle the kitchen." When the younger women watched her, immobilized, she said, "Come on, ladies. Get a move on. We have work to do." From where they were waiting in the hallway, Doreen grabbed the mops, buckets and cleaning products.

A while later, Lori surveyed her bed, the bed Jack had used. She wasn't sure she could sleep in it again. She was saying those words aloud to herself when Doreen entered the room.

"Nonsense, my dear," she said. "Of course you will. That bed is just fine." She tugged off the sheets with a glare into the living room at Ellie, who was supposed to have done that. "The sheets are washable or you can decide later to buy new ones. Look. The mattress is just fine, not a stain on it. You take good care of your things, don't you?"

"I used to although you'd never know it today."

They were partly through and the place was starting to look like someone might have lived there, when a knock sounded on the door. Doreen answered to admit Millie, Mel and Ben's housekeeper.

"When Ben told me what happened I came right over to help," Millie said. "Hi, Lori. I'm so sorry this happened to you, dear." She reached for the mop in Lori's hand. "Give it to me."

Lori's newfound independent streak popped into place. Sure, she'd been shell-shocked during her shower but this was her place. Time to take back control. "Look, everyone. Thank you for your kindness, but I'm all right now. I can finish up…"

She was interrupted by Mel who grabbed her arm, and propelled her into the bathroom. "I know this is an invasion of your privacy, another invasion on top of what already happened. But look at my mom and at Millie." She opened the door a crack so Lori could peek out. "I haven't seen Mom so happy in years. She's taking charge. She's looking after her kids and their friends. Let's let her, please Lori. We'll be out of your hair soon then you can decide what to do."

Looking at the amount of progress the women had made in such a short time, Lori relented. It would have taken her days to make this much dent in the mess if she tried on her own. Accepting some help didn't necessarily mean she was a wimp or letting other people govern her life, did it? With a deep breath, she gave Mel a hug, a "thanks" and left the bathroom.

On cue, Doreen said, "Lori, there you are. It's decided. You're coming home with me."

CHAPTER 13

Lori gaped at Mel and Jeff's mother.

"We're not going to have things in shape enough for you to sleep here tonight. The laundry's not done and I'm sorry dear, but they broke every dish you own and made a mess of your food." She waited for Lori's look of shock to recede. It didn't, so she continued. "Pack a small bag and come home with me, just for tonight. You'll have something to eat, sleep in a clean bed and have some time to think. You can't stay with Ellie - her place is no bigger than this. Mel and Ben don't have a spare bedroom. I have lots of room."

Lori hesitated. She looked around, wanting to reclaim her own space but it was evident that the place was not habitable yet. She could camp out here but was proving a point worth the discomfort? Behind Doreen's back Mel nodded at Lori and gave her a thumb's up. That was the signal they used in class when they were on the right track.

She tried to inject warmth into her tone. "Thank you so much, Mrs. Nicols. I'll take you up on your offer."

"Are you sure this is all right?" Lori felt funny taking over Jeff's bedroom, even if he did sleep downstairs now.

Of course. Mel's room has my sewing things spread out, while Jeff moved most of his things downstairs. This gives you space to bring some of your things from your apartment."

"Thanks, but I'll just be here for the night. I should have my place straightened out tomorrow."

"You're welcome as long as you'd like to stay."

Supper was one the table within minutes of Mr. Nicol's return home from work. It wasn't exactly what Lori expected. Boiled frozen vegetables added color to the baked pork chops. Seasonings were salt, pepper and a sprinkling of dried paprika. This was quite different fare than from what Jeff prepared at the bakery.

Curious, Lori asked him, "Did you mother teach you to cook?"

"Goodness no," Doreen replied. "I can't abide anyone else in my kitchen. He makes such a mess, you know, dirtying every pot in the house. And have you tasted his stuff?"

"Pucker your taste buds," Mr. Nicols added.

"I was on my own in this," Jeff said.

"He watched those cooking shows incessantly then would want to use my kitchen for his experiments."

"Mel was more tolerant of my efforts and let me use her kitchen once she moved out," said Jeff.

"Can you cook?" Doreen asked Lori.

"All right, but I'm not in Jeff's league."

"Good," said Doreen. "If you hook up with my son, you'll have to do all the cooking if you want to eat solid, plain cooking."

Lori's head came back and she looked from Doreen to Jeff. "But we're not, I mean, we're...". She looked helplessly at Jeff.

He regarded her with interest. "Go on. We're what?"

"It's not like that," Lori tried to explain. "We're friends."

"Only way to start out," threw in Jeff's dad as he returned to eating.

Lori spread the classified ads on the kitchen table. The cleaning in her place was finished, the bed was usable, she could buy new dishes and there were always more garage sales for the rest of the things. But somehow, the place didn't feel the same. It had lost the feeling of a haven for her and she was not sure she could ever get that back.

Jeff came up the stairs and asked what she was doing.

"Checking the classifieds for apartments to rent, but there's not much here."

"Why are you using that? Who uses the newspaper anymore? Owners have to pay to list their places in the paper. Come with me. I'll show you how it's done."

Downstairs he pulled up online after online site listing places in their city. The databases were searchable with whatever parameters Lori wanted and there were far more possibilities online than appeared in the paper.

They copied the information on the most promising ones, printed them and then set out to look.

Lori wanted light. While she liked trees, anything too shadowed blocked out the sunlight and would not work for her. The size of the kitchen didn't matter as she wasn't that into cooking. One bedroom would likely be all she could afford, although two would be better. Ideally, the place would be close enough to school that she could walk to work much of the time. She also liked neighborhoods where she could walk for groceries and feel safe doing so. Oh, and yes, she needed a big, soaker bathtub, preferably one of the old claw footed types.

Modern high rises were out, both for price and aesthetic reasons. To Jeff, four walls were four walls. Once he understood Lori's housing parameters he was quickly able to analyze each potential place, ruling it out when it didn't meet all the things Lori said she wanted.

"Wait a minute," Lori told him. "There's something about this building that appeals to me."

"But it doesn't have the high ceilings you said you needed."

To Jeff, this didn't make sense, and he thought Lori's rules were pretty iffy. He trailed after her though.

"It's a maybe but not quite perfect." Lori decided. As they walked to the next place, she noticed that Jeff was quiet. He was never one for chit chat but usually they conversed comfortably. Now, he looked pensive. "Everything okay, Jeff?"

"Yeah. I'm just thinking. Maybe it's time I got a place of my own and moved out of my parents' basement."

"Why haven't you?"

"It's easy. It has everything I need. There's plenty of space for my computer stuff, it's warm and dry. No one bothers me. And, it makes my mother happy."

"She looks pretty healthy. Does she need you to be close for safety reasons?"

"Huh. Safety for me she'd say, not for her or my dad. They're okay on their own and doing pretty well for old people. Dad's coming close to retirement age in a few years.

"Mom worries about me - this Asperger's thing, you know. I had a bad experience when I tried college. It was too much and I got overwhelmed and had to quit. Well, I didn't have to quit, I guess. I chose too."

"You're a smart guy. What was so difficult?"

"I told you a bit about it before, you know about executive function? That's often a tough area for people on the autism spectrum. I had trouble organizing myself, doing all the readings and assignments for five classes at once, going to classes at all different times. That's different than high school where you go and you're in class solid from nine to three or so. At college, my class schedule was erratic and the rooms were located all over. I got mixed up often.

"Mel tried to help, but I wouldn't listen. I thought I could do it. And, I likely could have if I'd used some of the strategies she told me about."

Lori nodded. "You're not the only person to get overwhelmed at college. I certainly did. It probably happens to everyone."

"But you don't have autism on top of all the juggling everyone has to handle. Try sitting in a lecture theatre with three hundred other people, listening to someone talk on and on when you have auditory processing problems. There were so many distractions. I should have seated myself right at the front like Mel suggested, but I didn't. Between me and the Prof, there were so many bodies that would squirm and squeak their chairs and turn their pages and make scratching noises with pencils. It was all I could do to make out what was being said and impossible for me to listen, understand and take notes at the same time. There were ways around this, but I didn't try any of them."

"So you flunked out?"

"I had great marks in some classes, like my computer science ones, but they make you take all sorts of classes. The ones I liked I did the work. I ignored the boring ones." Jeff looked sideways at Lori. "It doesn't really work that way, does it?"

"Nope. So you never got your degree." It was a statement, not a question.

"Oh, I did, just not from that college and not quickly. I pretty much did nothing for a couple years. I call that the licking my wounds period. Then I finally listened to my sister about online classes. Ah. They were made for guys like me. I could take one at a time and go through it at my pace. One by one I picked them off, loving some, hating others but I pushed through. So yes, I do have a degree. That's what helped me get all the contracts I have."

"Is that lucrative enough to be able to afford your own place?"

Jeff laughed. "My online contracts pay well. The income is sporadic, depending on the number of contracts I have going at any one time, but over a year I bring in quite a bit more than Mel makes teaching."

"What makes you think about getting your own place now?"

"Looking with you. Seeing how you feel about having your own space. And, maybe it's just time. Hey!" He grinned at Lori, "Maybe I've grown up."

Lori linked her arm with Jeff's. "I think I grew up this week, too."

Lori gave notice to her landlord that she'd be moving out at the end of the month. The pressure was on to find a new place; she couldn't bunk in with Jeff's parents forever. He offered that she could sleep downstairs. He would be up most nights coding and she could take his bed. Lori had no idea how she'd explain that to his parents, so declined. She knew that Doreen already wondered about the relationship between her son and Lori. Lori wondered about it, too.

Jeff texted Lori at school just as classes were dismissed for the day. He'd been apartment hunting for himself but kept an eye out for something that might fit Lori's exacting requirements. For him, things were simpler. He needed upgraded wiring with lots of plugs to handle all his computer equipment. And he needed a decent kitchen - a very decent kitchen. Other than that, little mattered. He'd found though that when she helped him look, Lori found things he'd overlooked, things that might bug him once he moved in.

He thought he'd found a suitable place, the main floor of an older Victorian house. It was pricey, beyond what he'd hoped to pay, but the one bedroom looked perfect for his equipment with built-in shelves, lots of floor space and good blinds to keep out the glare from the direct sunlight. The owner said an electrician had redone all the wiring so that the old house was now up to code.

Although he liked the apartment, he wasn't sure. Jeff wanted Lori's take on it. Somehow, in the past month, he'd come to rely on her opinion.

"Sure. I'll meet you there in about thirty minutes," Lori agreed.

Jeff was sitting on the steps waiting for her, key in hand. "I put down a fifty buck deposit just to get to hold onto the key for the day," he said.

Lori didn't reply. She stared at the painted lady two storey Victorian with gingerbread trim and a deep wrap-around veranda. "What part of this are you thinking of renting?"

"The main floor."

"So this would be your entrance door?" She gestured toward the oversized wooden door with the crinkle glass sidelights and the clear transom glass overhead. "And this porch would be yours?"

"I suppose so. I didn't ask about that."

"No one else uses this door?"

"The owner lives on the top floor. Her entrance is at the side of the house. Why? Do you see a problem with it?" He gestured at the door and porch.

"Problem? I love it! This is the kind of place I've been looking for. Let's see the rest."

The door opened into a six foot wide hallway with dark, gleaming, hardwood floors. To the left was a living room. The bay window was skirted with built-in seating. A carved mantle topped the brick fireplace on the side wall, with matching oak bookshelves on either side. Lori spun around and around taking in each detail. She pointed at the high, coffered ceilings.

Jeff followed her point, squinting. He couldn't see anything wrong. There was a storey above them, so there shouldn't be water stains from a leaking roof. "What's wrong?"

"Wrong? Nothing. This place is gorgeous."

Jeff didn't know about gorgeous but he did know about the kitchen. He grabbed her hand and pulled her back through to the other side of the hallway. "Come look at this."

The kitchen was as large as the living room, which meant at least three times bigger than Lori's previous kitchen. In addition to the double sink, there was a smaller bar sink in the center island. Granite counter tops shone under the spot lights Jeff switched on. The five burner gas stove looked new. Jeff thought the fridge could be larger, but its pull-out bottom freezer compartment looked spacious enough to Lori. While there was no eat-in kitchen table, four tall, wicker-backed stools were drawn up to an eating area overhang in the island. Jeff demonstrated the built-in cutting boards and showed her the storage areas for all his kitchen gadgets.

While Lori didn't wax on as Jeff had hoped about the kitchen, she was over the top when she inspected the bathroom. It had her requisite claw-foot soaker tub, an electric towel warmer on the wall, along with a heating bulb positioned over the tub. An oval-shaped shower rod circled the ceiling above the tub and a shower faucet was on the end wall. The old-style pedestal sink offered no storage room, but the double linen closet certainly did. There was even a carved oak table at the side of the tub to hold her lotions and bath salts and a candle or two.

Oh, wait, thought Lori. This place is for Jeff, not me. He likely doesn't light candles when he soaks in a bubble bath. She smiled to herself.

Jeff didn't find bathrooms all that imaginative so he took her hand to pull her to the most important room - his computer space. He detailed where he'd place each component, showed her how nice and dark it was with the blinds pulled so there would be no glare on his monitors.

"It's a one bedroom?" she asked.

They set off to see the last room in the suite. Jeff waited in the doorway while Lori waxed on about the beauties of this last room. The corner windows faced both south and east, bringing in the kind of light she loved, the same light there would be mornings in the living room. There was no closet, but there was a free-standing wardrobe. Shelves were built around the radiator along one wall, the bottom ones deep enough to almost serve as a table. One part of the shelving was closed, with a handle and a latch. Lori pulled and it dropped down to reveal a desk. Lori's eyes went again to the coffered ceiling. Jeff didn't get what difference the nine foot ceilings made or the border around them. He didn't bonk his head on the seven foot ceilings of his parents' basement.

"It's perfect. Just perfect," Lori assured him.

"You don't find anything the matter with it?"

"Maybe one thing. What's the price? A place this gorgeous must be out of this world."

She winced when Jeff told her. "That would be out of my budget - half again as much as I could afford."

Jeff looked confused. "I was thinking of this place for me. Don't worry. I'll keep helping you look until you find the perfect place."

I think I have found the perfect place, Lori thought to herself.

CHAPTER 14

Jeff ran the key upstairs to the landlady. After a couple minutes, Lori ran after him. She wanted to meet this woman as well. Maybe the landlady would be the fly in the ointment. Otherwise this place was too perfect.

Nope, the landlady wouldn't be a hindrance. She was sweet. When their kids were young, they'd used the whole place. When their children grew up and moved away, her husband had renovated the place, turning the upstairs into a self-contained suite that they rented out. Now that her husband had passed away, Naomi found the downstairs too big for herself. Plus, she could get more rent for it. She invited Lori and Jeff to tour the upstairs. A glassed-in veranda sat atop the one off the first floor. Lori hadn't even noticed the door between Jeff's computer room and the bathroom that opened onto the back deck. Did this place have even one flaw?

Naomi drew in a breath and looked from Jeff to Lori. "There is one stipulation I have. Whoever rents the first floor must also look after the yard. My Doug used to do that, but I hate yard work. Just detest it. So I need someone who will cut the grass, do some weeding and if so inclined plant a few flowers - generally keep the outside tidy." She waited. "Are you up for that?"

"Yes!" Lori said. "Yes, definitely. I love gardening but haven't had much chance living in apartments."

Jeff brow furrowed. He turned to Lori. "You'll come over to look after my yard?"

Lori took his arm with her left hand and stuck out her right to Naomi. "It was nice meeting you. I think Jeff and I need to go talk a bit more."

The walked around to the front of the house and sat on the porch steps.

Lori could see how the veranda could look with overflowing pots of flowering plants, a porch swing, a couple Adirondack chairs....

"I have an idea," she started. "You need a place to live. I need a place to live. This place has all the things you were looking for. It has all the things I was looking for." She waited.

Jeff nodded, but admitted he hadn't known it was what she wanted as well.

"So?" Lori asked.

What? Was she wanting him to back off and let her have the place because she liked it so much? She'd said she couldn't afford the rent. "You'll have to help me here. What are you getting at?"

"It's a two bedroom place. It's on the expensive side, but if two people shared the rent, it would be totally affordable. We're friends. I think we could get along okay as roommates."

"Roommates? You mean like we should share this place?"

Lori nodded, less sure of herself. She'd thought it was a great idea, but Jeff was not warming up to the thought the way she did.

"A roommate. I've never had a roommate before." He faced the porch step, raising just his eyes to her. "I'm different than other people. I like to stay up all night working. I like it quiet when I work. I like to cook and will spend hours in the kitchen. Just ask Mel. I'll take over hers for the whole day sometimes. She doesn't really mind, because she gets to eat everything I make and I'm a very good cook."

"Sounds fine to me."

"Are you sure? There's more. I don't like anyone messing with my computer stuff. I arrange it just the way I like it."

"I have my own laptop. I don't like to cook, but I do like to eat."

Jeff tried to think of more objections, but none came. This might work. "Okay."

"Okay? Just like that?"

"We just went over the potential problems, didn't we?"

"Okay. It's a deal, then."

"Deal." Jeff held out his hand for Lori to shake.

She grabbed his hand, and then pulled him tight for a hug. "Thanks, Jeff. This will be wonderful." Jeff patted her back awkwardly, afraid to let himself move too close or read more into the gesture than Lori intended. A woman like Lori interested in him? Nah. They were friends and he was lucky to have that much.

The next few weeks were spent readying for the move. Since most of Lori's second-hand furnishings had been destroyed by Jack and his buddies, she had little to pack and move. What she wanted to keep was stored in boxes in Mel's basement. They'd hoped to put them in the Nicols' basement but with Jeff's array of computer stuff and his fear of getting his components knocked, they'd opted for Mel's place.

They salvaged what they could of Lori's belongings, but she had a hard time looking at them. Jack had sullied the place for her. As well as feeling the need to move away, Lori wanted a fresh start with her material possessions as well. She kept most of her clothes and a few personal things, but started anew with the rest. The originals had come from garage sales and second hand stores. There were plenty of those around for her new round of shopping.

Since neither of them owned furniture, Jeff and Lori shopped together. Jeff's main requirement was comfort, so Lori did the choosing. While Jeff had kitchen equipment galore, he had no dishes or cutlery of his own. They bought new, this being the only kitchen area where Lori had free rein. Mel was glad to see Jeff's culinary accouterments leave her kitchen, creating extra space for the more mundane things she liked to use. Some had also been stored at the bakery and Ellie was relieved to no longer have to work around them.

Pretty much every moment not spent at their jobs at school or the bakery was spent together. Taking each other's hands as they shopped became natural. Never had Jeff felt as relaxed with someone else, someone who knew when to talk and when to just be companionably silent. Lori had pursuits of her own she enjoyed and often spent evenings curled up with her Kindle, reading on Jeff's lounging chair - the one she'd slept on that first night, while Jeff worked on his computer programs.

Sometimes she'd just sit and watch Jeff, marveling at his concentration and how his fingers flew over the keyboards, his eyes darting from screen to screen. His focus was intense. Lori often felt that after a full seven hours at school, her work was done for the day. Many days Jeff spent eight hours at the bakery, came home and worked long into the night on his contracts for coding, web site management, regression testing, quality assurance or a host of other things she couldn't follow when he did try to explain. When she asked how he could work like that, he said it was easy when you love what you're doing.

Mel, Ben, Rob and Ellie left. They'd spent the day helping Lori and Jeff move into their new place, setting up the furniture and hanging drapes. Jeff allowed no one to help him arrange the kitchen; that was his territory. He concentrated on that first thing and stuck to that room, leaving the rest to do the heavy work throughout the rest of the suite. Ben and Rob quit grumbling once the aromas drifted out of the oven. Jeff was cooking for them. Ben offered to come move them anytime as long as he'd get to eat like this.

Now, evening was here and their helpers had departed, leaving some

Alexander Keith's and a lovely bottle of merlot behind.

Mrs. Nicols was right; Lori's bed was salvageable. In fact, with new bedding, it was as good as new. Her queen size bed fit well into the bedroom, leaving plenty of room to walk around. Lori no longer had to jump up onto the bed to reach any of her clothes. In fact this bedroom could hardly be any better. Her belongings fit neatly into one half of the wardrobe and the larger of the two dressers.

She left her room to see how Jeff was making out in his computer office. Cables ran everywhere. The shelves were laden with component pieces Lori had no clue about. The hum of computer cooling fans was audible. She was used to that now, the sound a part of Jeff being at home. "How's everything fitting?" she asked.

"Great. I'm almost done here. This is even better than in mom's basement. There's no carpet and the shape of this room is perfect for wheeling my chair around. See?" He demonstrated how he could move from screen to screen.

Lori backed into the hallway and rested her hand on the thin, older single bed mattress resting against the wall. "What about this?"

Jeff poked his head out and looked at the mattress in dismay. "My bed. I forgot all about it." He surveyed his room. "There's no room. How will I get that in here?"

He took off for the living room. It wasn't overly full of furniture but what there was was comfortably arranged. "Maybe if we pushed the couch and chair together...," he suggested.

"Nope. Oh, no. Our living room is perfect the way it is."

"Then where am I going to sleep?"

Lori took his hand. "I have an idea." She pulled him into her room and pointed at her bed.

"But this is your room."

"Yep." She went and sat on the bed, then held out her hand to him.

It took Jeff a bit for her meaning to register, causing Lori some angst. Oh, god, she thought. Now I've ruined it. Maybe I misread things and he only wants to be friends.

Jeff regarded her intently. "Are you sure?"

Again, she said, "Yep."

Jeff turned around and she feared he was about to refuse and leave. "Be right back," he said as he returned to his room down the hall. Lori heard the sound of switches going off, and then the humming sounds lessened. He returned to the doorway and grasped the door handle. Lori held out her arms, Jeff smiled and went to her, after closing the door behind them.

THANK YOU

Thank you for spending this time with Karen, Rita, Jeff and Lori. If you have enjoyed this story, the author would be greatly appreciative if you would leave a review at this link: https://www.amazon.com/Autism-Talks-Book-School-Daze-ebook/dp/B01IIUZH3S. Reviews mean a lot to authors.

Author Dr. Sharon Mitchell loves connecting with readers. Contact her through her website at http://www.drsharonmitchell.org. There you will find information on her other books her workshop appearances and questions families and teachers often ask about kids who have autism spectrum disorders.

Turn the page to see the other books in the series.

Other Books in the Series

There's more! If you liked Autism Talks and Talks, you might also enjoy the other books in the series. Each focuses on a different child who has an autism spectrum disorder. Many of the same characters appear in each book.

Here's a synopsis of each book:

Autism Goes to School

We're thrilled to announce that this Amazon bestseller is also a B.R.A.G. Medallion winner!

After suddenly receiving custody of his five year old son, Ben must learn how to be a dad. The fact that he'd even fathered a child was news to him. Not only does this mean restructuring his sixty-hour workweek and becoming responsible for another human being, but also Kyle has autism.

Enter the school system and a shaky beginning. Under the guidance of a gifted teacher, Ben and Kyle take tentative steps to becoming father and son.

Teacher Melanie Nicols sees Ben as a deadbeat dad, but grudgingly comes to admire how he hangs in, determined to learn for his son's sake. Her admiration grows to more as father and son come to rely on Melanie being a part of their lives.

When parents receive the news that their child has autism, they spend countless hours researching the subject, usually at night, after an exhausting day. Teachers, when they hear that they'll have a student with an autism spectrum disorder, also try to learn as much as they can. This novel was written for such parents and teachers - an entertaining read that offers information on autism and strategies that work.

Bonus Section
At the back of the book are links and references useful to parents and teachers.

> You can find Autism Goes to School FREE at these retailers:
> Amazon.com
> BookHip.com/ZPHDQC
> iTunes
> Kobo
> Barnes & Noble paperback
> Barnes & Noble e-book

What Are Reviewers Saying About *Autism Goes to School?*

- "A gem of a book"

- " A true delight - Highly, highly recommended

- Just couldn't put it down"

- "Highly informative and extremely helpful - Couldn't take my eyes off it"

- I loved this book from beginning to end - Just plain awesome
- I could feel the author's passion - What a great way to learn about autism

- "Entertains, entrances & educates: 3 for the price of one!"

- "This wonderful book is about a Dad, Ben, meeting his autistic son Kyle for the very first time, when Mom dumps him suddenly on his doorstep, saying she can no longer take care of him. Through the eyes of Ben, we get a glimpse of both the challenges and joys of being a parent of a child who sees the world in different ways."

- "Unlike some stories that speak of autistic children, this one brings a wealth of hope and information! As we look over Ben's shoulder, we see a glimpse of the learning tools currently being used in the classroom today, and we get glimpses of things that could be helpful in the day to day life of an autistic child."

- "I appreciated this story on several levels. First I enjoyed the story of Ben discovering what it means to be a parent, especially a single parent. Second, I enjoyed watching Kyle find his own means of success in this new and upside down world."

- "I enjoyed the glimpse into classroom life and options available today. Finally I enjoyed the quiet romance between Mel and Ben."

Autism Runs Away

Ethan is only in grade one and already has been *kicked out of one school* due to his tantrums and pattern of running away when in a panic. Now, his mom's enrolled him in a new school but remains glued to her phone, waiting for the call to tell her to come pick him up, that they can't handle him, that they don't know what to do with a child who has autism.

How can she trust these strangers to look after her son, just one small child among hundreds, when he has run from own parents so very many times? They don't know the terror of losing your child in a mall or watching him run blindly into traffic.

What started as a fun chase game when Ethan was a toddler has turned into a terrifying deviation. The adults in his life never know when he might take off.

Rather than attaching an adult to his side to keep him safe, this new teacher talks about calming strategies and choices. Do they not realize what could happen if Ethan flees the building? The impact of a car on one small body? Sara is about to learn if this new school is up to the challenge.

Meet Kyle, Mel, Ben and the other characters you got to know in the Amazon bestseller Autism Goes to School. See what they've been up to in the last year and how they join forces to help Ethan.

Go to this link for free sample chapters in all formats: BookHip.com/ZPHDQC.

You'll find Autism Runs Away on Amazon at https://www.amazon.com/Autism-Runs-Away-Book-School-ebook/dp/B01FCYQ7DC

Autism Belongs

Manny is not like other children. He doesn't talk. He doesn't leave the house. His parents desperately try to arrange their world so that Manny does not get upset. Because, when he does, well, the aggression was getting worse. Too many times Tomas had to leave work to rescue his wife from the havoc of their son's meltdowns. At ten, Manny was becoming difficult to handle.

Passing by a bakery made all the difference. There, they met people who understand autism, along with its strengths and challenges. They learn ways to help Manny communicate and socialize and to have his needs met.

Dare they consider letting him go to school? Is there a chance that Manny actually belongs there? You bet

Meet Kyle, Ben, Mel and the other characters you read about in the Amazon bestseller *Autism Goes to School* and see how they've grown and progressed.

For free sample chapters (in all formats), head to: BookHipcom/ SGCVFJ.

You can find Autism Belongs on Amazon at this URL: https://www.amazon.com/Autism-Belongs-School-Daze-Book-ebook/dp/B0184ZQMI6/.

Autism Talks and Talks

Karen is a grade 6 student who has Asperger's Syndrome. She is bright, vivacious and highly verbal. Too verbal. She finds certain topics fascinating, studies them in-depth and is all too willing to share her knowledge with others. She goes on and on and on, not realizing that she is boring and alienating the other kids with her endless monologues. Her protective mom tries to shield her from the world, limiting her contact with peers in case she might be bullied.

Karen would like to be social. She remains on the fringe, looking at other adolescents having fun together and wondering if she could ever be a part of the group.

Karen has potential. Her inability to read body language and her lack of knowledge in social pragmatics get in the way of interacting with others her age and having friends. Through a structured group at school, she begins to understand the give and take of conversation and to have some positive experiences with her peers.

And, can a young man with Asperger's find love?

For free sample chapters (in all formats), head to: BookHip.com/ LTGFAB.

Autism Talks and Talks is on Amazon at https://www.amazon.com/Autism-Talks-Book-School-Daze-ebook/dp/B01IIUZH3S

Autism Grows Up

At twenty-one, Suzie has withdrawn from a world she finds alien and confusing. Ability is not the problem, nor is interest – many things fascinate her. But, she has Asperger's Syndrome and high anxiety. To her, the world is a harsh, scary place where she does not fit.

Suzie lives with her mother, Amanda. She spends much of her day sleeping and most of her nights on the computer. Her mom wishes Suzie would get a job, go to school or at least help out around the house. Suzie feels that her time is amply filled with the compelling world lurking within her comp.

Amanda has two full time jobs – one involves working at the office every day, the second involves looking after Suzie. Amanda wants more for Suze, but does not know how to help her move forward. When she tries putting pressure on her, Suzie suffers from paralyzing anxiety, resulting in morose withdrawal or worse, lengthy tantrums. Suzie is most content when alone in the basement with her computer. Staring at her monitor, the rest of the world falls away and she feels at home.

Amanda is torn. She met this gentleman, Jack. It would be nice to spend time with someone other than her brother and daughter but Suzie wouldn't like it and she needs her mother desperately. Amanda's brother asks uncomfortable questions like what will become of Suzie if something happens to Amanda.

Jack gently persists and Amanda glimpses what her life could be like. Suzie resents the time her mom spends with Jack and makes her mother pay for the hours not devoted to her daughter.

When, they have a home invasion Amanda has only Suzie to rely on.

For free sample chapters in all formats, head to this link: BookHip.com/ KSGVSC.

Autism Grows Up is for sale on Amazon at https://www.amazon.com/Autism-Grows-School-Daze-Book-ebook/dp/B01JB8QW3U.

Autism Goes to School Workbook

Readers who followed Ben and Kyle's journey in Autism Goes to School have said that they would like a guide to help them follow the strategies that Ben and Kyle try. Of course, not every strategy works for everyone. Remember that once you've met a child with autism, you have met one child with autism. While we're all unique, there is often a core cluster of characteristics that kids on the spectrum share.

The workbook looks at the things Ben did right and the mistakes he made, despite his good intentions. It looks at Kyle's responses, then guides you to consider how your child with autism might respond.

There is space to profile your son, daughter or student's strengths and the areas that pose the most challenge right now.

The guide will help you look at the sensory issues that might contribute to the difficulties and ways to help. It discusses the communicative aspect of behavior and how you can help the child better express his wants and needs in appropriate ways. A self-regulated child is a calmer, happier child.

There are examples of visuals and schedules and space to create your own. And, there is an extensive list of references that will help you guide your child to be as independent as he can be.

The Autism Goes to School Workbook will be available on Amazon in 2017.

Prequel to Autism Goes to School

Readers have asked about the lives of Jeff and Mel prior to Autism Goes to School. Coming in 2017 you can read their stories. Go along with Jeff to his first try at college and living away from home. Follow Mel's path as she learns more autism spectrum disorders. Learn about the struggles as their family struggles with the balance of protecting Jeff and fostering his independence.

This Prequel will be out in 2017.

A free Advanced Reader Copy will be sent to those on the Review Team. To join the Review Team, leave a message for Dr. Mitchell at http://www.drsharonmitchell.org.

And, of course, you can get your FREE copy of Autism Goes to School in all formats here: BookHip.com/ZPHDQC.

ABOUT THE AUTHOR

Dr. Sharon A. Mitchell has worked as a teacher, counselor, psychologist and consultant for over thirty years. Her Master's and Doctorate degrees focused on autism spectrum disorders. She has delivered workshops and seminars to thousands of participants at regional and national conferences.

Sharon loves connecting with readers. Contact her through her website at http://www.drsharonmitchell.org. There you will find information on her other books her workshop appearances and questions families and teachers often ask about kids who have autism spectrum disorders.

Join the mailing list at http://www.drsharonmitchell.org to be informed when the next book will be released and to find freebies and sample chapters. Follow her Amazon author page at http://www.amazon.com/Dr.-Sharon-A.-Mitchell/e/B008MPJCYA/ref=ntt_dp_epwbk_0.

www.ingramcontent.com/pod-product-compliance
Lightning Source LLC
Chambersburg PA
CBHW050601300426
44112CB00013B/2024